TRUE BUMS

by

James Russell

"If you love trains, you'll love True Bums!"

Copyright 1995 #Pau1-835-916 by James Russell all rights reserved. James Russell Publishing printed in the USA. www.powernet.net/~scrnplay Pre-press version April 1999 Published Edition October 2001. ISBN # 0-916367-26-6 (Print Version) ISBN # 0-916367-43-6 (e-book Version) Library of Congress Card Number - None.

To locate publisher type in; "James Russell Publishing" in any Internet search engine. The original script is 118 pages. This publication required a few extra pages due to pre-publishing formatting and typesetting requirements.

DEDICATION TO:
"It is a good thing to give thanks unto the Lord." Psalm 92.1

A THOUGHT TO PONDER:
There are over 800 promises in the Bible. Have you read them?

FADE IN:

EXT. SKY OVER SAN FRANCISCO BAY - DAY   PRESENT

Helicopter descends to a fog cloud. THREE MEN in business
attire dangle upside-down from ropes tied to ankle and skid.
Helicopter dissolves in fog.

EXT. GOLDEN GATE BRIDGE - DAY

Traffic crushes to a stop as chopper blades pound the air
into submission. Car HORNS blare, faces in cars furious.
THREE MEN drop to pavement and untie ropes. One of the men
is black.

Chopper wash kicks road grit. Irate DRIVERS can't exit cars.
Some try, but are severely sandblasted. Paint peels,
windshields pit.

Chopper veers under the bridge. Wind dies. Drivers rush out
of cars to kill those three guys.

SIRENS wail, motorcycle COPS shimmy through tightly packed
cars, flashing blue lights alternate. More bikes race up
sidewalk, gaining fast.

The three men climb railing, stand hand-in-hand. Just as cops
and drivers grasp their coats, they leap YEOW! Cops hold
coats, lean over railing to see,

Three men fall, tumble, SCREAM. Three parachutes unfold
under shirts, float to a container ship.

BLACK PARACHUTIST POV

Six legs frantically kick the air. Ship's mast approaches
like a giant hypodermic needle. Panicky CHINESE MEN on ship
YELL, wave hands to steer away. Ship's HORN blows. Pointed
tip of the mast goes right up between his legs.

                    MAN IN PARACHUTE (V.O.)
                  (Black man, Texas
                   accent)
            Ohhh, damn!

DISSOLVE TO BLACK

Sound of pants RIP! YEOW!

INT. PSYCHIATRIST OFFICE - DAY

DICK CROSSMAHEART (40) flat on couch. He's one of the men we
saw jump off the bridge. If he were an actor he would be a
star. Briskly rubs forehead, panic attack victim. DOCTOR
(30) leans over Dick. Dick picks his thumb.

                          DOCTOR
          Dick Crossmaheart, why did you?

                          DOCTOR
                    (continuing)
          I told you it will entirely make
          your condition worse. I can't
          treat you if you won't listen to
          me.

                          DICK
          I can't help it. It's no fun
          being rich anymore. I hate it!
          I'm going crazy, Doc. The only
          deeds keeping me sane is doing
          stupid things, but I can't hold
          out much longer. I'm slipping.

Dick's flailing hands desperately grasps Doctor's shirt
sleeve, bunches it into a tight fist.

                          DICK
                    (continuing)
          I worked like a canine all my
          life. Work, work, work my fingers
          raw to the bone for my parents
          were poor. Where did my youth go?
          Why did I get married?

Pulls shirt hard. Slowly starts to tear.

                          DICK
                    (continuing)
          She did it. Didn't she? She
          stole my youth! I want it back.
          I'm desperate, Doc. I'm afraid of
          getting old. There has to be a
          cure, you hear me, there has to
          be. Give me a pill, a shot,
          anything. Cuuure meeeee!

Doctor pry's Dick's fingers. Dick tightens grip.

                          DOCTOR
                    (terror in eyes)
          It's a mid-life crisis. Life is
          too long to be miserable. It
          won't last. Let go of me!

Dick pulls harder, tears Doctor's shirt, clutches his white
coat. Doctor backs up, shirt and coat rips. Dick holds with
a white- knuckle grip. They scream at each other.

                          DICK
          I'll give you all my money if you
          make me happy. I want to be young
          again. I need a life I want to live.

                         DOCTOR
              Did you see the psychic I told you
              to visit?

                         DICK
              She refused to see me. She said
              she knew I wouldn't pay the bill.

Angry Doctor grabs Dick's shirt with both hands, tears it
away, exposes Dick's hairy chest.

                         DICK
                    (continuing)
              I'm too good to die!

SECRETARY enters,

                         SECRETARY
              Oops, sorry.

EXT. RESTAURANT / ENCINO - LATE AFTERNOON

DICK and the TWO MEN we saw on the bridge in business suits
sit under umbrella covered table, loudly sip coffee. BLACK
MAN is DONNY BROOKS (35). He's a tall Texan, wears white
cowboy hat. CLIFF MORALS (25) short, unsure of himself,
Boston accent.

WAITRESS grants them defiled looks. ELDERLY COUPLE dressed as
farmers sit close by, listen.

                         DONNY
              No, no, no. I don't like it. Tie
              the bitch to the bed, then make
              her eat dog food.

                         CLIFF
              It didn't work.

Cliff picks a red bite wound on his arm. A pigeon pecks
Donny's shoe, he kicks it AWK! Pigeon bites his arm and
leaves OW!

                         DICK
                    (chuckling)
              Sounds like you need to learn how
              to manage women.

Elderly couple and offended CUSTOMERS leave.

                         OLD WOMAN
                    (Southern draw, to
                     trio)
              Ye'all should wash yawl mouth out
              with turkey poop!

Elderly couple leave. A bald MANAGER approaches trio.

                    MANAGER
          That does it. You guys are fleas
          in a rat's groin looking for
          misfortune. Scattered my
          customers again. Out of here!

Waitress smiles, flicks finger against arm as if flicking a
flea. Dick frowns, smirks to Manager as he pick his thumb.

                    DICK
          C'mon guys, this lil' pooch has no
          hair.

Manager's face red as a beet, waitress giggles. Trio leaves,
Donny limps.

                    DONNY
          I left more than my heart in San
          Francisco.

Waitress checks table for tips, lifts a penny, winds-up like
a baseball pitcher.

                    WAITRESS
          If you want good service, serve
          yourself!

Penny whizzes past trio's heads. Slaps a storefront window
PING! Penny falls to sidewalk, spins and HUMS like a top.

BUM, SAM SIMMONS (50) in filthy rags strolls by, picks up
penny, gazes at window, sees, "Bank of Hollywood" staggers
inside.

MOMENTS LATER

SIMMONS exits. MANAGER escorts, all smiles.

                    BANK MANAGER
          Thank You, Mr. Simmons. Come
          again, sir. I'll personally
          assure your account is handled to
          your complete satisfaction.

Manager happily waves as Simmons steps into a silver Rolls
Royce. License tag, "Rich Bum."

EXT. OFFICE BUILDING / BURBANK - MORNING

TRIO walks on busy sidewalk. Everyone greets them as VIP's.
They are. Office building - "Universe Pictures, Inc."

DICK, DONNY and CLIFF wear gold chain belts. Dick accidentally steps on a BUSINESS MAN'S long watch chain, jerks him to an abrupt stop. Man loses balance, falls down.

     Bus pulls to curb. Dick lifts the man up with a tug of his chain. Man angrily brushes his clothes.

                         BUSINESS MAN
               Hey, watch what you're doing
               clumsy fuzz-ball nincompooper.

                         DICK
               I'm really sorry.

                         BUSINESS MAN
               I ought to sue you for cruelty!

                         DICK
               Sue my wife. She has all my
               money, to the dime.

Dick picks his thumb.

                         BUSINESS MAN
               You defiled my chain. Ruined my
               suit, scuffed my shoes, and --

Dick sidesteps to bus. Man's terrorized face as Dick hooks Man's chain to bicycle rack on bus rear bumper.

Bus leaves, drags the SCREAMING man backwards. Blue smoke stream from heels. Nobody notices, nobody cares. Railroad tracks in b.g.

Old bearded HOBO wrapped head-to-toe in gold chains lies against steps. PEOPLE drop coins in the donation can PLINK! PLINK! Hobo doesn't smile.

                         DICK
               That's what life can do to you.
               Some people have so many burdens
               it incapacitates them.

Trio drop coins into can CLINK! Enter building.

INT. UNIVERSE PICTURES / HALLWAY - DAY

Foxy SECRETARIES with scripts in arm flirt to TRIO. Each wear unique colored chains on waist, ends sway like a tail.

CHARLOTTE (30) with armful of scripts doesn't smile. DICK grabs her chain, yanks her to a stop. She's bewildered, off balance.

                         DICK
               You're new I gather?

                     CHARLOTTE
            First day. I'm looking for Mr.
            Crossmaheart's office. I'm his
            new assistant secretary.

Dick extends a handshake.

                     DICK
            You're looking at him. Welcome
            aboard.

Charlotte fumbles scripts to free a hand. She shakes Dick's
hand, obviously finds him attractive.

                     CHARLOTTE
            I'm Charlotte Bridges. You're the
            Chief Executive Officer? The big
            man in Hollywood I hear.

                     DICK
            I like to think so, but sometimes
            I wonder about that. Call me,
            Dick. This here is Donny
            Brooks, Vice President.

DONNY kisses Charlotte on nose. She giggles, rubs nose.
Other SECRETARIES passing by sneer.

                     DICK
               (continuing)
            This here is, Cliff Morals.

CLIFF nods his head. Charlotte nods. Cliff's mesmerized,
stares into la la land. Charlotte's blouse dragged by heavy
scripts in arm, a Grand Canyon cleavage.

                     DICK
               (continuing; joking)
            Cliff is Hollywood's best unknown
            story analyst.

                     CLIFF
               (to Dick)
            Story editor. I'm almost finished
            with Invasion of the Grannies
            script, but I need a secretary,
            today. Like right now!

                     DONNY
            I demand to have her.

                              DICK
                         (to Donny)
                    You have six of the best, Donny.
                         (to Cliff)
                    She's yours until the grannies
                    capture Los Angeles, then she's
                    mine. A deal?

Cliff nods. Charlotte's suspicious. Donny fondles the tail
of her chain, link-by-link, gets close to her rear. Charlotte
yanks chain away, slaps Donny's hand OUCH!

                              CHARLOTTE
                    I've heard of the Hollywood
                    shuffle. I bet you guys have a
                    casting couch too?

Dick's flabbergasted.

                              DICK
                    Rumors, ugly rumors. Listen
                    Charlotte, Hollywood is full of
                    bull dung and buffalo chip
                    stories. This is tinseltown and
                    it's entirely built on lies.

                              CHARLOTTE
                    Your lying?

                              DICK
                    Okay, people in hell shouldn't be
                    allowed ice water. Would you
                    believe --

STEVEN SPELLBOUND (40) in coat and tie approaches, he's
excited.

                              MAN
                    Excuse me. Dick? Steven
                    Spellbound. "Invasion of the
                    Grannies" script, it's better than
                    the comedy, "Grandpa Beats-up the
                    Congressmen". I'll do it, but you
                    know the part when the three men --

Dick covers Spellbound's mouth with hand.

                              DICK
                    Tsk,tsk. Trust me. Will you trust
                    me? People are ready for this
                    film. Will you direct it? For me?

Spellbound rubs chin, nods approval. Dick removes his hand.

                         DICK
                     (continuing)
                 Green light. It's a go!

INT. PACIFIC PALISADES HOME / DEN - SUNSET

Sun melts into ocean. DICK stands by open window. Matrix
printer spits out spreadsheet in b.g.

Expensive cars enter driveway below. Dick's disgusted. Rich
WOMEN exit cars, talk gibberish, giggle. Voices louder,
women now in the house.

                     WOMAN'S VOICE (V.O.)
                 Dick? They're heeere.

Dick snaps off computer, glances to oil painting of Tom
Sawyer fishing by a river. Walks downstairs.

INT. DINING ROOM - SUNSET

Lavish tea party as you'd see in the White House. WOMEN hold
tea cups. A six-tier cake with fifty gold candles sits on a
twenty-foot table.

DICK approaches cake. Frosting reads, "Congratulations Dick
$50 Million!!!" Dick's wife YVONNE (38) gazes with
expectations of joy, but receives a blank expression.

She whispers to Dick as he picks his thumb.

                         YVONNE
                 Don't you embarrass me. They
                 believe we are happy. Fake it. Be
                 a good hubby, blow the candles.

Yvonne affectionately pinches Dick's cheek as her foot
crushes his toe. Dick grins, pecks her on cheek, takes a
deep breath, blows out the candles.

Whipped cream flings on ladies gowns, cake falls.

                         YVONNE
                     (embarrassed)
                 I'm sorry. With fifty million I'm
                 sure Dick will buy you all new
                 gowns. Right, sweetie?

Women grasp vibrating cups, angrily stare at Dick. He waves
good-bye as he exits front door. Door slams.

EXT. DECK - DUSK

Dick leans on railing, sees distant highway. Red and white
lights of cars - a river of jewels winding through a dim
forest. Sweeping white strobe light. PULSATING locomotive
engines rise in volume.

INT. UNIVERSE STUDIOS / DICK'S OFFICE - MORNING

First floor suite. Skinny secretary ELISE TIPPY (70) busily
enters and leaves Dick's office, stacks scripts on his desk.
DICK sits, watches the pile grow like a weed.

                    ELISE
          The best way to beat a mid-life
          crises, Dick, is to not think how
          rotten life really is.

Dick stares with puppy dog eyes. Elise shoves another stack
of scripts on desk. Stack leans, Dick's hand steadies them.
She pats his hand a couple times, leaves, closes door.

Dick picks his thumb.

Dick's overwhelmed. Folds his hands into a knot, elbows on
desk, head dives to fists, prays.

                    DICK
          Empty is the life filled with
          nothing but things. Show me the
          way. I'll do anything you ask of
          me, go anywhere you want me to go.
          Deliver me from this evil world --

Diesel locomotive HORN blast interrupts. He opens window,
sees freight train pulling boxcars. Steel wheels SQUEAL,
blast of compressed air PSSST! Brakes grind.

Train stops 100-feet from window.

                    DICK
                 (continuing)
          That's odd. Trains never stop
          here. Look at all that raw power!

Three engines thump on idle, sporadic PSST! of compressed
air. Black haze of smoke float from exhaust vents. KIDS run
to the engines.

ENGINEER waves. Dick leans out window, waves. CHILDREN look
to Dick and wave. Dick waves.

Door slides open on blue boxcar, "Pacific Turnip Express."
Dirty HOBO slowly waves arm in a circular motion. Dick's
stunned. Kick of smoke rise from engines VAROOM!

Dick's eyes glance to heaven.

                    DICK
                (continuing)
          You must be joking?

HORN blows. Puffs of dense smoke shoot into the sky. Roots
engine blowers WHINE. Deep exhaust tones pulse as train
leaves, metallic CLACK, ZINGS of steel compressing steel
fills the air.

EXT. UNDER DICK'S OFFICE WINDOW - DAY

Drunken WINO propped against wall lazily waves to HOBO in
boxcar, swigs wine bottle. Hobo waves to him to board the
train. Wino passes out.

WIDER VIEW - DICK joyfully waves to hobo in boxcar, believing
the hobo is waving to him.

INT. DICK'S OFFICE - DAY

Dick leans out window. ELISE enters, SCREAMS. DONNY and
CLIFF charge into office, grab Dick's pants, rip them down,
reveals Mother Goose imprints.

                    DICK
         Hey! What's going on here?
         Clifford, I'm ashamed you would
         succumb to such perversion!

Dick conceals himself behind chair.

                    CLIFF
         Why do you want to kill yourself?

                    DICK
         Kill myself? I was just leaning
         out my window watching the train.
         What's wrong with you guys? I'm
         on the first floor, six-feet up.

                    DONNY
         Well it did look like a suicide
         attempt.

Dick pulls up his pants.

                    DICK
         You stooges been watching too many
         movies.

                    ELISE
          The first symptom is denial. Then
          it's a desire for sympathy, then
          they kill themselves. That's what
          my husband did during his mid-life
          crises. But he's okay now.

Dick, Donny and Cliff gaze at Elise.

                    ELISE
                 (continuing)
          That's the cure, you know?

EXT. OUTDOOR RESTAURANT - DAY

TRIO eat lunch on Ventura Blvd. BUS pulls to curb. Exhaust
pipe pumps acrid brown diesel fumes on them.

BUS DRIVER exits, hails a taxi, leaves. Dick inhales fumes.

                    DICK
          I love the smell of diesel in the
          morning.

Donny and Cliff gag, eyes squint. People dining COUGH and
rub eyes as they eat.

                    DICK
                 (continuing)
          I've had it with responsibilities.
          Why do we continue to work for a
          living? To satisfy our wives lust
          for vanity? That's why. It's
          slavery. Men need freedom!

Donny flips page of an adventure magazine.

                    DONNY
          We never did float the Amazon with
          innertubes.

Dick grabs magazine, throws it, lands on MAN'S plate. Man
throws it to Dick, misses, hits WOMAN'S face. Woman throws
magazine back at man, spills his coffee.

                    DICK
          That's what I'm talking about.
          We've done it all and frankly, I'm
          bored stiff. We're always looking
          for thrills, but it doesn't last.
          We need to do what we really want
          to do. I'm not talking about
          vacations. Chuck it all. Live
          free as the wind blows.

Man throws his wallet at woman. Woman's bra flies past
Dick's face.

                         CLIFF
                    (gags on coffee)
                You mean leave our families and
                jobs, permanently?

Donny ducks as jockstrap sails by his nose.

                         DICK
                Exactly. The ultimate adventure.
                To live like Tom Sawyer,
                Huckleberry Finn. Stepping into
                the twilight zone. Escape from
                L.A.

Woman throws bagel at man, sails by Dick's nose, smacks side
of the man's head.

                         DONNY
                Every man's dream, uh-huh? Log
                cabin in the forest, go fishing
                everyday, live off the land, free
                of all encumbrances.

                Sounds good, Dick. It's
                impractical in the real world.
                You'd give up everything to be a
                bum? Go see a shrink.

Man throws pie at woman, splats her breast.

                         DICK
                Where's your imagination? The
                wives can stay home and take care
                of things. We have money, plenty
                enough to take care of each other.

Cliff and Donny bored, eyes roll up.

                         DICK
                    (continuing)
                What I'm saying is there is life
                before death. Many dying grooms
                express disappointment in life.
                Their dreams never became reality.
                Never accomplished what they set
                out to do and suddenly, it's over.

Woman throws panty-hose at the man face. Man notices phone
number written on it. They smile, join hands and leave.

Dick points to a Norman Rockwell of Tom Sawyer, barefooted, fishing by a river bank on menu. As he stares into drawing,

THE DREAM

EXT. COUNTRY WATERHOLE - DAY

He's a BOY (10) swings from a rope, splashes into water. Swims to shore, climbs embankment on hands and knees. Other BOYS do likewise.

As Dick grasps edge of embankment, he latches onto a heavily scuffed wingtip shoe. Looks up, sees unshaven OLD MAN (58) angrily stare down at him with willow branch in hand.

Old man grabs Dick by the hair, pulls him to his feet, squeezes his arm tightly, slaps Dick on the head twice, hard, Dick stumbles OW!

> OLD MAN
> My son ain't gonna end up like
> these scum. Git, I said, git in
> the house. Ya got work to do,
> boy. I'll put ethics in you yet.

Whacks Dick with willow branch on behind YEOW!

> DICK
> (crying)
> But papa, I only want to have fun
> with my friends. Papa, papa.
> Please, don't hit me --

Father grabs Dick by earlobe, slaps his head YAAAGH! Kids stop playing. They stare as Dick is dragged away.

> OLD MAN
> Don't you ever talk back to me
> boy. I know what's best for ya.
> Git in the house and study. You
> is gonna be a successful man if I
> have to whip your brain --

Father's raises hand with stick to strike Dick's butt.

BACK TO SCENE

DICK shaken, rubs his butt, picks his thumb. Donny and Cliff smile with serenity at the painting. MANAGER throws a BUM out by the collar

> MANAGER
> Get out! Lousy freeloader.

PEOPLE board bus. Little OLD LADY wears Casey Jones hat, hops in drivers seat, guns throttle, rear wheels smoke patch of rubber. Dense diesel fumes pour on PATRONS. Patrons gag.

INT. CLIFF'S HOME / KITCHEN - DAY

DEBBIE MORALS (30) on phone, changes BABY'S diaper on kitchen
table as CLIFF eats.

                    DEBBIE
          Oh, oh, mom. It's only a few
          days. Cliff hasn't had a vacation
          in two-years. I could use a break.

Debbie slides soiled diaper near Cliff's plate. He pushes it
away. Unconsciously, Debbie slides it back. Cliff stares at
diaper, then his meal, loses appetite. A poodle BARKS o.s.

                    DEBBIE
                  (continuing)
          Thanks, mum. I love you too.

KELLY (9) barges in front door, explodes with excitement.

                    KELLY
          Mommy, daddy, look. The
          Bradford's have a brand new car.

Cliff's jaw hardens, slams fork down, races to front door,
sees NEIGHBORS exit an expensive gold car.

Cliff exits front door.

EXT. ACROSS THE STREET / BY BRADFORD'S HOUSE - DAY

CLIFF approaches BRADFORD FAMILY. Their home beautifully
landscaped.

BOB BRADFORD (30) dressed in white shirt, shorts, shoes with
neon orange laces. Well-dressed BRADFORD FAMILY stand by new
car.

Neighborhood KIDS, shabby clothes, flock to car. Cliff peeks
inside car, kicks tires, wipes finger along rooftop.
Bradford's POODLE nips at Cliff's pants OW! He kicks at the
dog.

                    CLIFF
          Very nice, Bob. Don't you feel
          any sense of shame or guilt?

                    BOB BRADFORD
          I was like you once, working my
          jackass off and where did it get
          me? Nowhere. Don't whimper to me
          for sympathy. You can do the same,
          but you're chicken.

                    CLIFF
          I have principles to live by.

MRS. BRADFORD hands silver spoons to her CHILDREN. They use
them as lollipops.

                    BOB
          You don't see my wife or my kids
          wearing rags do you? I want my
          family to be happy. Those are my
          principles.

Kelly tugs on Cliff's pants.

                    KELLY
          Daddy? Can we have a new car too?
          Pleeese.

                    CLIFF
          Someday, Kelly. Someday, we will.

                    BOB
          Don't kid yourself, Cliff.
          Someday never comes. Times are
          changing. Only working people get
          stiffed. Look, it's easy to get
          on the welfare train. You'll love
          it. It's a charmed life.

Cliff's home is a wreck along with the entire neighborhood.
Dilapidated cars line the street, some on jacks without
wheels.

DEBBIE stands by front door, hands on hips. Hands in
pockets, Cliff sulks home. Bradford's poodle pees on his leg.

                    KELLY
                 (to poodle)
          Don't you pee on my Daddy.

Poodle flashes teeth, GROWLS. Kelly runs home. Dog YELPS
delightfully as Cliff and Kelly enter the house. Bob
WHISTLES to dog.

                    BOB'S VOICE (V.O.)
          That's a good girl. Yes, you're
          a good girl, aren't you? C'mon
          poochie, I got a special treat for
          you today.

Bob carries his wife across threshold, his wife BARKS like a
poodle.

EXT. DONNY'S HOME / MALIBU - DAY

High society WOMEN lounge by pool. CHRISTINE BROOKINGS (37)
black, long fingernails, entertains guests.

DONNY exits home in underwear, cannonball plunges into pool.
Water soaks guests. He splashes, spits water on them, laughs.

Christine snatches him by earlobe. Donny's underwear floats
to surface as she yanks him out of the water.

> CHRISTINE
> (Southern accent)
> You get in that house and work on
> your movies. I'm sick'n tired of
> your antics. This ain't no comedy
> flick. You're an eternal
> embarrassment to me!

Christine leads him by the ear into house. Women's eyes
reveal enjoyment, but they play it up.

> WOMEN
> (random whispers)
> "That's disgraceful." "So
> uncouth." "I feel sympathy for
> Christine."

EXT. RAILROAD TRACKS / BY UNIVERSE STUDIOS - MORNING

TRIO stand on tracks. CHARLOTTE and ELISE approach, tug
their belt chains.

> ELISE
> Dick Crossmaheart? You get back
> into the office right now. You
> have work to do.

> CHARLOTTE
> Clifford Morals? Donny Brookings?
> You heard the lady.

> DICK, DONNY, AND CLIFF
> (simultaneously)
> I'll be there in a minute. I just
> want to watch the train.

Locomotive horn HONKS in the distance. White oscillating
strobe flickers bright as the sun.

Charlotte and Elise drop the chains, angrily stomp back to
office, footsteps pound the earth THUMP! THUMP! THUMP! Train
closer, HORN shouts warnings.

Three SD-40 diesels belch black smoke. THUNDERING assault of
3,000 horsepower. HORN blasts force trio off the track.

Engines idle down, brakes SQUEAL. Compressed air blasts
their hair as engines glide by PSSSSS! Bell rings DINGALING!

Train stops. A short train of four dirty brown boxcars with
red caboose. CONDUCTOR in a beautiful black uniform steps
from engine cab to engine platform.

ENGINEER wears Casey Jones gray/black stripe hat, smiles as
he swivels chair looking to trio.
                    CONDUCTOR
                  (formally)
          All aboard!

Trio gaze at each other with unbelieving eyes. Boxcar door on
"Lima Bean Freight Line" slides open. The same HOBO Dick saw
earlier, stands, waves his arm, invites someone to board.

BUM arrives, hobo helps him climb in. Hobo smiles at trio.

                    CONDUCTOR
                  (continuing)
          Last call. All aboard!

Engineer pulls bell lanyard, DINGALING! DINGALING! Triple
horns blow. Hobo extends open hand, smiles.

                    DICK
          This is it boys. I'm going.

Dick grasps hobo's hand, pulled aboard. Donny and Cliff
exchange looks.

                    DONNY
          What the hell. Wait for me!

They climb aboard. HORN blows, compressed air released PSSST!
Engines wind up VAROOM! VAROOM! Train creeps forward.

INT. LIMA BEAN BOXCAR - DAY

TRIO stand by doorway. CHARLOTTE and ELISE run from office to
train. Engines step up a notch VROOM! VROOM! VROOM! Trio
wave, train accelerates.

EXT. BY TRACKS - DAY

CHARLOTTE and ELISE shake fists, SHOUT, frustrated.

                    ELISE
                  (to Charlotte)
          You need to learn that a man will
          invariably run from his
          responsibilities at the first
          opportunity if you don't keep a
          tight grasp on his chain.

INT. LIMA BEAN BOXCAR - DAY

City view slips by boxcar door. CLICKITY-CLACK of wheels,
rocking motion, gives us a sense of a joy ride.

                     HOBO
            Welcome aboard. I knew it was
            only a matter of time you would
            come. It happens to the best of
            us. My name is, Frank Wiener.

They shake hands, introduce each other.

                    FRANK
            This here is my dear friend,
            Harry. Descendant of, Jed Young.
            The first bum to stowaway on a
            California wagon train.

Harry fiddles with a gold chain on neck that droops into
shirt.

                    CLIFF
            I read about that. So many bums
            hitched rides under the wagons of
            the Donner Party it slowed them
            down. They couldn't get over the
            Sierra's before the winter
            snowstorms.

Donny cautiously looks out the boxcar door. He gets dizzy.

                    HARRY
            That was Jedediah Smith, not Jed
            Young. He did it in 1828. My
            great, great, great grandfather
            got blamed for that.

Donny crosses over to a Coke machine. Presses "Coke" and
Champagne bottle drops, hits machine with fist.

                    FRANK
            His grandfather was the first bum
            to rob the Virginia and Truckee
            Railroad. The infamous strong
            armed robbery in Verdi, Nevada.
            A highway plaque on interstate
            eighty honors the event. First
            train robbery west of the
            Mississippi.

Donny steps up to group, faces Frank.

                    DONNY
            Is that right? That was your
            relative, huh?

Harry still fumbles with the gold chain, he mumbles, gazes
down into his shirt. Cliff advances a curious look.

                         HARRY
                     (nonchalantly)
               Well, it's no big thing. Really.

Cliff still eyeballs the gold chain in Harry's hand.

                         CLIFF
               Where's this train going?

Harry turns, Cliff can't see. Cliff's neck stretches.

                         FRANK
               No place, to nothing, to nowhere.
               Anywhere you need to go. A man
               need not know his limitations.
               Not here, in the good life.

Dick frowns, walks around the dirty boxcar.

                         DICK
               Good life? Living in squalor you
               call this the good life?

Frank and Harry laugh, point to his chain.

                         FRANK
               Nothing to chain us here. No
               responsibilities, no worries, no
               commitments, no bills to pay.
               Yeah, it's the good life all
               right. Don't you say, Harry?

Harry snickers, nods head. Trio examine belt chains. Harry
removes boltcutter from under a crate.

                         FRANK
                     (continuing)
               If you do, life as you know it
               will no longer exist. There's no
               turning back.

                         HARRY
               A fool wanders, but a wise man
               travels.

Frank takes boltcutter from Harry, waits for decision. Trio
huddles. They argue, then,

                         DICK
               We need to keep our credit cards.

                         FRANK
               That's not a problem.

Frank snaps chains with tool. Trio exhilarated, leap like
kids. Harry hands them oily ropes, trio tie-up their pants.

                    CLIFF
          I feel like a weight is lifted
          from my thighs.

                    DICK
          Oh gosh, this is great.

                    DONNY
          Free at last! Free at last!

     HONK! Train enters street crossing, arms drop DING! DING!
     People in stopped cars wave. They wave back.

EXT. R.R. TRACKS BY UNIVERSE PICTURES - DAY

     CHARLOTTE and ELISE, frantically point up tracks. SPELLBOUND
     sees a distant caboose disappear over a small rise.

                    CHARLOTTE
          They jumped that train with dirty
          hoboes.

                    SPELLBOUND
               (aghast)
          I don't believe it.

                    ELISE
          I knew something was brewing when
          that freight train kept stopping.
          I've lived here seventy-five years
          and never beheld the likes of it.
          We should report it to the police.

     Charlotte nods approvingly.

                    SPELLBOUND
          We should, but you won't.
               (to Charlotte)
          Neither will you. They are just
          up to their old antics again
          seeking a thrill, getting a story
          idea for their next film. They'll
          be back.

     Charlotte adjusts her bra. Spellbound's brows rise. She
     smiles, he smiles.

                    ELISE
          Not this time. I know men. They
          want freedom. Bums at heart,
          that's what I say. They want to
          live like Huckleberry Finn, toss
          everything away and just do
          nothing. If it were not for us
          women nothing would ever get done!

     Charlotte nods approvingly.

INT. LIMA BEAN BOXCAR - DAY

Train rolls north along San Fernando road. TRIO and FRANK
sit at doorway, dangle bare feet in air.

DONNY sits far left. HARRY sits in hay inside boxcar, hand
in shirt, vigorously scratches armpits.

>   FRANK
>   Gentlemen. I'm afraid we can't
>   allow you to meet our associates
>   dressed like that.

>   DICK
>   What's wrong with these clothes?
>   Bought these threads from Sacker's
>   Boutique, Wilshire Boulevard.
>   Eighteen-hundred smackers. Can't
>   get much better in Hollywierd.

>   FRANK
>   Not appropriate attire for the
>   occasion. You shall look like a
>   bum if you inspire to be a bum.

>   HARRY
>   He's saying, ya gotta look like a
>   bum if ya wanna be a bum. Get rid
>   of the zoot suits.

Tree branch magically sweeps over DICK, CLIFF and Frank's
feet, swipes Donny's right foot OUCH! Donny sucks sore toe.
His left foot dangles outside with the others. Nobody
notices Donny's misfortune.

Frank hands Dick black graphite grease. Dick and Cliff
reluctantly rub grease into fabric.

>   CLIFF
>   My next door neighbor's a bum,
>   collects welfare and he don't look
>   like a bum.

>   FRANK
>   He's not a real bum. A true bum
>   never begs, hitchhikes or asks for
>   handouts. They don't cheat
>   people, or lie. A hobo would, but
>   not a true bum.

Frank scratches chin, eyes lift in deep thought.

>   FRANK
>   (continuing)
>   Well, stealing, hmmm. We fancy to
>   declare we borrow commodities.

> HARRY
> Don't forget the knees, ya gotta
> rip the knees.

Frank hands Dick a knife. Dick slices pants knees.
Tree branch swipes Donny's left foot OUCH! Donny pulls foot
inside, sits with both knees to chest, busily rubs sore feet.

> DICK
> Bums have their own code of ethics?

Harry frantically scratches armpits, giggles, talks to
himself. Cliff stares at him.

> HARRY
> Darn tootin'. Don't forget the
> aglets. Ya gotta fray'em.

Dick frays the ends of his shoelaces.

> DICK
> Interesting. Laws in the Kingdom
> of Bumdum. I want to get away
> from rules.

> FRANK
> They ain't rules, laws or anything
> like that. It comes from the
> heart. Respect for one's brother.

> HARRY
> Or sister.

> DICK
> Sister? Women bums?

> HARRY
> Bumlarinas, tramps. Call'em what
> ya like. Rare, but they do exist.
> Women's lib caused it. They don't
> last long, we see to that.

Donny nervously peeks out doorway. BIRD crashes into his
face. Bird's feet snagged in Donny's hair, angrily pecks
ear. Both SQUAWKING. Nobody notices, nobody cares.

Frank, Cliff, Dick, shimmy inside boxcar. Cliff sits by
Harry. Donny struggles with bird in b.g. Cliff's nose
wrinkles.

> HARRY
> (continuing)
> You don't like my cologne? It's
> Oil of La Bete Puyant. Very
> expensive. Made from a stinking
> beast.

Aghast, everyone eyes meet.

                    CLIFF
          You have scabies?

                    HARRY
          Naw, just having some fun with my
          little buddy, Siphonaptera.

Harry removes gold chain around his neck, hands it to Cliff.
Attached is a small glass vial. Cliff's eyebrows sink as he
reads label, "Pet Flea". Small flea leaps inside.

                    HARRY
                 (continuing)
          That's, Marie. She plays a little
          rough sometimes. I think she
          likes you. Go ahead, take her for
          a spin.

Cliff opens bottle, flea jumps in his hair.

                    HARRY
                 (continuing)
          Uh-oh, you shouldn't have let her
          jump in your hair. It'll be a
          real bitch getting her out.

Cliff feels Marie biting OUCH! He scratches scalp so hard
clumps of hair cling to his fingers.

                    CLIFF
          Harry, get her out of my hair!

                    HARRY
          She's pissed off because I haven't
          let her out in over a month.
          She'll calm down in a day or two.

Cliff dunks his head in bucket of water.

                    HARRY
                 (continuing)
          She can swim. That will only make
          her frisky. She's a tropical
          flea, loves water. Here, try this.

Harry gives Cliff a lit cigarette and mirror. Cliff chases
Marie with cigarette all over his body.

Dick and Frank stand by door, look to locomotive chugging a
curve. San Fernando road below. Vehicles slowly pass by.
Dick and Frank oblivious to Donny and Cliff, despite painful
cries OW! OUCH! OUCH!

                    FRANK
          You will see things you never see.
          Dimensions known only by a chosen
          few.

Frank holds a can of red jelly fuel, canned heat.

                    DICK
          You're drunk. Drinking too much
          of that jellied napalm?

Dick sees a family in mini-van. KID in back seat wipes snot
on seat. ANOTHER KID pulls earwax from ear. HUSBAND drives,
flicks wrist trying to fling bugger off finger. WIFE pulls
a stringy white snot with tweezers from her nose. Dick
fingers his nose.

                    FRANK
          You're a blessed man, Dick
          Crossmaheart. You've been given
          a chance to see our world the way
          no one has seen it before.

                    HARRY
          It's the best kept secret in the
          universe.

Harry sneezes hard into his hand.

                    HARRY
               (continuing)
          Particles of comestibles
          forcefully ejected from the rhinal
          orifice can tell you a lot about
          the quality of life you live.

Harry swishes his finger into his wet palm. Dick frowns.
Donny and Cliff stare.

                    HARRY
               (continuing)
          Look, small black particles. It's
          the smog from city air. Nitrogen
          oxide, ten-micron particulates,
          aldehydes --

                    FRANK
               (interrupting)
          My friends, you will forever be
          changed men.

Cliff, gazes at Harry's hand with disgust.

                  DICK
        Yeah, and you guys are angels sent
        to save me. I don't want to hear
        your babbling lies. I'm here for
        a little fun, that's all. I'll be
        here today, gone tomorrow.

Donny plucks ear wax from ear. Wipes it on his pants.

                  HARRY
        Don't tell him no more, Frank. You
        know what happened to the last guy.

Harry wipes hand on pants.

                  DICK
        Look fellows, I've worked hard all
        my life, all I want is to just get
        away from the noise, parties, the
        job. I don't plan to make a
        career out of this.

Cliff and Donny look hard at Dick.

                  FRANK
        It's your wife, isn't it?

Cliff, Donny and Dick are stunned.

                  DICK
        What are you, a fortune teller?

                  FRANK
        We know more than you can tell.
        A man is as old as he feels
        himself to be. Growing old is
        nothing but a bad habit. Age is
        a bad traveling companion.

Dick looks at Donny and Cliff, both shrug their shoulders.

                  HARRY
        Youth comes and goes like the wind
        blows. Old age isn't so bad when
        you consider the alternative.

                              DICK
                    Two broken down good-for-nothing
                    loafing hobo bums who wouldn't
                    know brass from cash, and you're
                    telling me how to live? Don't
                    preach your philosophy on me.
                    I've made more money than you
                    could earn in an eternity.
                    Phooey. Let me tell you both
                    something. Money talks, and I'm
                    talking. Don't pretend to me you
                    know what life is all about.

Frank and Harry laugh. Dick's insulted.

                              FRANK
                         (to trio)
                    Adversity makes men, and
                    prosperity breeds monsters. A
                    man's life does not consist in the
                    abundance of things he possesses.
                    You will be better advised to
                    watch what we do and listen to
                    what we say.

Donny and Cliff amazingly stare at each other, then look to
Dick.

                              DONNY
                         (to Dick)
                    They are full of wisdom.

Donny and Cliff bow and attempt to kneel. Frank stops them.

                              FRANK
                    My sons, you shall know wisdom
                    when you meet the high prophet.

Harry nods approvingly. Dick's unimpressed.

EXT. LIMA BEAN BOXCAR - DAY

SIX FEET dangle from boxcar in the wind. Feet withdraw,
opposing TRAIN at high speed SWISHES by.

EXT. AERIAL SHOT - DAY

Trains pass by each other on a curve. BUMS sleep along top
of box cars.

INT. LIMA BEAN BOXCAR - DAY

DICK stretched on couch. HARRY takes notes. FRANK hands a
pill to Dick. Dick fumbles a wad of bills.

                         HARRY
               It is easy when we are in
               prosperity to give comfort to the
               afflicted. Money will destroy
               you. It has no value here. Get
               rid of it before it gets rid of
               you.

                         DICK
               But the Devil dances in a empty
               pocket.

Billboard passes by, a Devil Ham advertisement.

                         HARRY
               Evil enters as a needle and
               spreads like a vine. A man with
               money is a slave.

                         FRANK
               The cost of freedom is always
               high. Money costs too much. It
               can't buy the necessities of the
               soul.

Frank takes wad of bills, places it in banana peel, tosses it
out doorway. Money flutters in the wind, the peel falls
short, lands on door's edge. Harry eats a white chocolate
candy bar.

                         HARRY
               If you dwell on yesterday you will
               have no today or tomorrow.

                         DICK
               I understand now.

                         HARRY
               But, there are dangers.

Harry spits chocolate out doorway, splats on car windshield.
Upset PEOPLE in car point finger upward to a BIRD.

                         HARRY
                       (continuing)
               Many never return.

Cliff vigorously scratches armpit.

                         CLIFF
               I'm not so sure I want to go.
               Marie is ruining my trip.

                         FRANK
               You're welcome to step off.

Cliff peers out doorway, sees a deep ravine. Donny peeks out, slips on banana peel, dangles over edge.

                    DONNY
            I said I'd go!

EXT. RAILROAD TRACKS - NIGHT

- - THREE WOMEN in fine gowns stand within rails. We don't see faces, but they appear familiar. Engines distant, pulsating strobe flickers on rails like silver laser beams. Women eerily glow and fade to darkness with strobe pulse.

- - Train closer. Strobe intensifies. THUNDERING diesel engines fill the air. Ladies raise arms to stop train.

Train bears down. Strobes very intense.

- - CHAUFFEUR by limousine near tracks panics, steps away as POUNDING engines advance. Soft breeze caress ladies dresses. Locomotive closer, air horns frantically blow HONK!

- - PSSSSS! SCREECH! Gold sparks fan from brake pads along entire length of train. Expression of horror on ENGINEER and FIREMAN.

ENGINEER POV - Ladies, hands in air, struck by train.

WIDER VIEW - Darkness, train rumbles by. Caboose red light fades into the night.

Chauffeur flips on limo headlights, sees shredded clothes, bloody body parts scattered along tracks.

LIGHTS ON - SPELLBOUND in boom camera mount.

                    SPELLBOUND
            Cut. I'll buy that!

INT. CHRISTINE'S KITCHEN - DAY

WOMAN'S high heel shoe nervously taps marble floor.

                    CHRISTINE (V.O.)
            I don't want your husband. I
            don't know where he is. He's
            probably --

WIDER - CHRISTINE in chair, on telephone. Garbled woman's VOICE from receiver. CHIMES ring. MAID opens front door. It's YVONNE, speaks into mobile phone. Sneaks up behind Christine.

                    YVONNE
            You like my husband, don't you.

                        CHRISTINE
              Not like you're insinuating.

Yvonne sees box of chocolate candies on countertop. She
flicks one out of the box, chews as she speaks.

                        YVONNE
              Hmm! Those nut'n chewy candies
              are good. You shouldn't eat so
              many of them, Christine.

                        CHRISTINE
              Candy? Chocolate? I don't touch
              the stuff.

Yvonne reaches in for another.

                        YVONNE
              Your ly...ing.

Maid enters, points finger. Christine swivels around.

                        CHRISTINE
              Why you li'l Beverly Hillbilly.

Yvonne and Christine put phones down.

                        YVONNE
                   (laughing)
              Dick told me you had a candy ass.

CHIMES ring. Maid turns, but DEBBIE, CHARLOTTE and ELISE
walk in. They hold mobile phones, go straight for the
candies.

                        CHRISTINE
              They really aren't my chocolates.
              Hey, don't eat them all.

INT. OFFICE BUILDING STAIRWELL - DAY

Racing up stairwell, heavy BREATHING, six-shoes SLAP wood
stairs. MAN walks downstairs, looks up, face reflects a
nightmare, he's trampled, SCREAMS, tumbles down.

WOMAN walks downstairs, her eyes expand, black gloved hand
snatches her collar, yanks her downward. She SCREAMS in
harmony with the other poor soul. OTHERS step aside, backs
hug walls, all terrified.

We stop, face a frost-windowed door. Black gloved fist
punches through glass, reaches inside, unlocks and opens
door. Step into hallway, terrified people freeze, some run.

A door at the end of long hallway. Walk, then run to it.
Heavy BREATHING o.s. People open office doors, see us
coming, chins drop, doors SLAM shut. Closer to door, run

briskly, breathing heavy, shoes POUND floor hard, CRASH
through door into,

INT. MENS RESTROOM - DAY

MEN at urinals spin around SCREAM. Spray urine on floor as
they scramble to stalls. Some slip and fall.

We're back in hallway, see another door. Run for it, going
to crash, but stop abruptly. On frosted glass. "Mc'Corkle,
Private Detective, Lic. No. OU812."

Door opens, MC'CORKLE (40) sits with feet on desk, smokes
cigar. Casually glances to wall clock, 1:10 p.m., looks to
us with tired expression. Desk, floor, piled with paperwork.

                    MC'CORKLE
              You're late.

WIDER VIEW - YVONNE, CHRISTINE, DEBBIE stand PANTING,
scramble to couch. Yvonne wears black gloves.

                    MC'CORKLE
                  (continuing)
              You gals are serious.

Wives nod in unison, grasp heaving chests. Mc'Corkle rises,
paces, rubs forehead, snaps a pencil, flings it to huge pile
of broken pencils on floor.

                    MC'CORKLE
                  (continuing)
              The hubbies took off on a choo-
              choo train and you want me to
              fetch'em, chain'em up and bring'em
              back home. Right?

Wives agree in unison, pull open blouses, wave magazines to
cool their breasts, GASPING for air. Mc'Corkle displays
flawless teeth as he smiles.

EXT. MOJAVE TRAIN DEPOT - DAY

Freight locomotives lined up everywhere. Some slow rolling,
slicing rails with ZINGING noise from wheel flanges.

Others parked with engines THUMPING on idle.

Sporadic BLASTS of compressed air punctuate the low pitch
background RUMBLE of engines. Impressive collection of raw
power.

THREE MEN in business suits walk a string of parked
locomotives coupled to boxcars, tankcars, etc. One of the
men is black. They walk toward us, cross string of rails to
parked train #917.

Engineer CASEY (30) wears clean gray coveralls, Casey Jones
hat, steps from cab, strolls platform, eyes intently fixed on
those three men. Menacing air hose in hand. Three men
attempt to board boxcar.

Casey whacks hose against side of engine POW!

> CASEY
> Not my train you don't! Go on,
> scram, beat it, get out of here!

Men hightail across tracks, jump on a slow train idling
through the yard. Casey shakes his head, eyeballs those men
as he steps back into cab.

INSIDE CAB - SPARKY (60) a bum, sits in Fireman's seat. Casey
tosses hose to floor, removes coveralls, reveals filthy
tattered clothes.

> CASEY
> (continuing)
> Depot dogs. Bad bums. Think they
> can ride my train.

> SPARKY
> Boy Casey, you sure fooled'em.

Casey digs fingernails into face, pulls off a rubber mask.
He's a BUM (50) with a scraggly beard.

> CASEY
> One thing I can't stand is a
> wannabe bum. Times are changing,
> Sparky. City people invading our
> way of life seeking thrills. We
> paid our dues. We earned the
> right to be bums. True bums.

Sparky nods approvingly with pride. Casey steps out on
platform, eyes to caboose, sees swinging red kerosene signal
lantern. Casey steps inside, sits in Engineer's seat.

> CASEY
> (continuing)
> Time to get out of this hump yard.
> Sanders on? Lets walk this baby
> to the high iron.

EXT. MOJAVE TRAIN DEPOT / NEAR #917 BOXCARS - DAY

TRIO, FRANK, HARRY huddle under boxcar on adjacent track. A
boxcar labeled "Kumquat Juice" on the 917 train. Harry
points.

> HARRY
> Home, sweet home.

INT. 917 ENGINE CAB - DAY

REARVIEW MIRROR - TRIO, FRANK, HARRY, sneak onto boxcar, each
carry a hobo stick on shoulder with burlap bag attached. Dick
dressed like Tom Sawyer.

Casey and Sparky don't see them. Casey flips air brake
levers PSSST! Red panel light shifts to green. Casey notches
throttle to #1 position VROOM! Sand flows on slipping engine
drivewheels.

Blowers WHINE add authority to the scene. On console, direct
current ammeter needle rises. Couplings take up slack KA-BOOM!''

Ties slowly sucked under locomotive, cab gently rocks, rails
compress and flex downward, loose ties GROAN.

Casey notches throttle to #2 VROOM! VROOM! VROOM! Vibration
RATTLES cab. Sparky and Casey grin as they see the
snowcapped Tehachapi mountains on the horizon. Breeze
ruffles their hair.

MUSIC similar to, "No Time To Kill" as train rolls.

                    CASEY
          Sacramento, here we come.

INT. R.R. DEPOT / CREW QUARTERS / LOUNGE - DAY

                    MECHANIC
          Hey, Jack? Your train leavin'
          without ya.

                    JACK
          Got it covered, Bob. Need to go
          to a wedding today.

Locomotives pass by window.   A BUM waves. Jack waves.

                    BOB
          Iron Face ever found out bums are
          drivin' his trains he'll yank ya
          license fo' sure. Federal Traffic
          Commission's crackin' down. Bums
          can't drive trains, Jack. They're
          causing too many derailments.

BUMS sit in boxcars as train passes. They wave.

                        JACK
          Bob, bums been drivin' trains for
          over a hundred years. Railroad
          has insurance and Fed's themselves
          are part-time bums. They ain't
          gonna change nothin'. Public'll
          never know what's going on. They
          assume it's an accident, that's
          all. FTC investigates, it's all
          covered-up. Business as usual.
          Truth'll never be known.

EXT. LOS ANGELES RAIL YARD - DAY

MC'CORKLE wears blue jeans, red/black plaid shirt under a
long overcoat. Walks a rail, loses balance. Ragged BUM (50)
on adjacent rail runs by. He wears black engineer boots.

                        MC'CORKLE
          Hey? How'd you do that?

Bum slides to a stop, swings leg around, turns to Mc'Corkle,
smoothly strolls back not missing a step.

                        BUM
          Comes natural in time. Can't step
          on nails, glass, oil, or
          chemicals, you know?
                    (beat)
          I didn't see'em.

                        MC'CORKLE
          See who?

                        BUM
          You're lookin' for somebody.

                        MC'CORKLE
          How do you know that?

                        BUM
          I thought so.

Mc'Corkle flashes his Private Detective ID card.

                        MC'CORKLE
          Okay, I am.

Mc'Corkle reaches into coat, extracts poster with Trio's
photographs, "Missing Children". Bum notices gun in shoulder
holster.

                        BUM
          I don't know them.

Bum twitches fingers. Mc'Corkle delivers $20 from a large
roll. Bum stares deeply into poster.

                    BUM
                        (continuing)
            My memory is fading. I'm old
            ya'know!

Mc'Corkle peels off two more. Bum looks over his shoulder.

                    BUM
                        (continuing)
            They haven't taken their vows so
            I can tell you. When they do. No
            bum can. They're on nine-one-
            seven to Sac.

                    MC'CORKLE
            Why Sacramento?

                    BUM
            Old Town. Celebrating one-hundred
            sixty-fifth steam days
            anniversary. Every respectable bum
            in the world attends. It's a
            venerable event. A true bum won't
            miss it.

Bum sees something, turns, fast-steps along the rail. He
takes a sharp turn on track switch, vanishes behind a parked
boxcar. Mc'Corkle folds poster, stuffs it to coat pocket.

BEEP! Mc'Corkle jumps, turns, sees rusty Ford convertible,
top down, bumper inches from his legs. Yellow rotating light
flashes. Tires decompressed to hug rails.

It's the RAILROAD POLICE. One in front seat, two in back,
all are old men (70's).

                    DRIVER
            Never stand on the road. Trains
            have a way of sneaking up on
            people. What's your business here?

                    MC'CORKLE
            Just strolling.

                    DRIVER
            You need to leave. We don't allow
            bums on the road.

Mc'Corkle, insulted.

                    MC'CORKLE
            I'm not a bum.

                     DRIVER
          And I'm not dumb! I've seen your
          kind before. I've been in this
          business fifty-three years. I'm
          telling you, mister. Don't do it.
          Go back where you came from.

Driver steps out of car. Mc'Corkle notices driver's brown
shoes are torn, heavily scuffed.

                     DRIVER
               (continuing)
          You'll freeze in winter, melt in
          summer. You think it's romantic,
          an escape to freedom, but it's a
          hellish life. You never know who
          will creep up on you, take your
          things, or your life.

Mc'Corkle eyes the two grumpy old men in back seat.

                  MC'CORKLE
          I'm dedicated. Since I was a boy
          I've loved trains. My heart won't
          say no. I got the requirements to
          be a good hobo.

Driver eyes the two men in back seat. They nod.

                     DRIVER
          Step inside. Maybe we can talk
          some sense into you.

Mc'Corkle hops in front seat. They crawl down the road. Bum
hiding behind boxcar watches. Inside car, trash items
scattered on floor, soda cans, chew tobacco, cigarette packs,
apple core, watermelon slices, bottle of champagne, etc.

Man in back seat behind driver taps Mc'Corkle on shoulder.
Mc'Corkle turns, sees man smile, reveals rotten teeth.
Mc'Corkle's smile reveals even worse.

                  MC'CORKLE
          Your teeth are like mine.

                     MAN
          I'm the fifth dentist.

                  MC'CORKLE
          The fifth?

                     MAN
          Four out of five dentist recommend
          Crusty toothpaste. I'm the guy
          who didn't recommend it.

                    DRIVER
          We know who you are.

The man grabs Mc'Corkle's hair, bends neck back over the
seat. Driver reaches into Mc'Corkle's coat, removes gun,
points it at temple.

                    DRIVER
                 (continuing)
          Give us your money.

Mc'Corkle struggles to remove money from pocket. Driver takes
roll of cash, throws money into the wind. Man lets go of
Mc'Corkle's hair. Gun now on bridge of his nose. Driver
tosses gun to tracks, slams the brakes, skids to a stop.

                    DRIVER
                 (continuing)
          Get out!

Mc'Corkle steps out, car leaves. Mc'Corkle, bewildered,
walks back, picks up gun. Engineer boot pins hand to gravel
CRUNCH!

                    A MAN'S VOICE (V.O.)
          Let it go and live.

WIDER - it's the bum we saw earlier walking on the rails.
Mc'Corkle lets go of gun, bum kicks it, lands on a rail.

                    MC'CORKLE
          It's you?

                    BUM
          Don't ask questions. Just walk
          real slow-like to that boxcar.
          Don't even think of running,
          there's others nearby.

They approach a rusty brown boxcar labeled, "Banana Fruit
Line." Door slides open a crack. OLD MAN (70) unshaven face,
peeks out. Eyes shifty, nervous.

                    BUM
                 (continuing; to
                 Mc'Corkle)
          Take off your shoes.

Mc'Corkle, baffled, slips off shoes. Door opens, they enter,

INT. BANANA FRUIT LINE BOXCAR - DAY

It's lavishly decorated. Pink wall-to-wall carpet,
chandelier, wet bar, kitchen, big screen TV. MC'CORKLE'S
stunned. OLD MAN is skinny, frail, struggles with champagne
cork, pours drinks. His name is SKINNER.

                          SKINNER
                   It's not Beverly Hills, but it's
                   home. I'm Mr. Skinner. What do
                   ya think about it?

                          MC'CORKLE
                   Oh, I'm Mc'Corkle. It's, it's,
                   beautiful. I thought --

                          BUM
                           (interrupting)
                   We live like tramps? Hoboes?
                   Transient vagrant panhandling
                   lowlifes? You've been watching
                   too many movies. Call me Jasper.

JASPER remotely flips on big-screen TV, sits in leather
recliner chair.

                          JASPER
                   Emperor of the North is on. Have
                   you seen it? Best flick Hollywood
                   ever made about bums.

Mc'Corkle wags head, sits in leather chair. Skinner hands him
champagne glass and pair of torn shoes.

ON TV - LEE MARVIN tells the kid, CIGARETTE,

                          LEE MARVIN (V.O.)
                   I'm gonna tell you once, so listen
                   tight, you got a chance to be a
                   good bum.

                          MC'CORKLE
                   Never saw it, but it looks good
                   already. How do you guys get away
                   with --

                          SKINNER
                           (interrupts)
                   Now you know why the engines run
                   all the time.

Skinner reclines on couch, lights corncob pipe.

                          MC'CORKLE
                   Engines? You lost me.

                          JASPER
                   Haven't you ever noticed
                   locomotives never shut down their
                   engines when parked?

                         MC'CORKLE
              Hmmm, I got it. Engine blocks
              will crack from thermal stress if
              you keep starting and stopping
              them.

Jasper and Skinner laugh.

                         JASPER
              That's what they want you to
              think, but the real reason is,
              they keep shutting them off and we
              keep turning them on. Railroad
              got tired of it so they just
              leave'em running. Been going on
              now for well over one-hundred and
              sixty-five years.

Convertible races by. Yellow light flashes. Train passes,
crushes Mc'Corkle's gun to a pancake.

                         MC'CORKLE
              You mean to tell me the railroad
              knows you guys exist?

                         SKINNER
              Of course. They leave us alone
              and we leave them alone.

                         MC'CORKLE
              How do you buy all this stuff if
              you don't work?

                         SKINNER
              Buy? Work? A true bum won't.

                         JASPER
              Everything's shipped by rail. We
              take what we need.

PSSST! Air released from brake cylinders.

                         MC'CORKLE
              That's stealing.

                         SKINNER
              It's payment for services we
              provide. Railroad writes it off,
              pays the manufacturer loss value.

Lights flicker momentarily.

                         MC'CORKLE
              Services? You work for the
              railroad?

                         JASPER
               Something like that. Human watch
               dogs. Our presence day and night
               keeps thieves away. A true bum is
               worth half a mil a year. We make
               the railroad money!

                         MC'CORKLE
               That's incredible.

Faint thunder rolling ever louder KA-BOOM! Boxcar shakes
violently. Mc'Corkle dives to floor.

                         JASPER
               Knuckles taking up slack. A minor
               inconvenience. Everything's
               bolted down tight. Is Borgnine or
               Marvin gonna be Emperor?

Train slowly creeps forward. Sound of GROANING steel as the
train's metal stretches from the engine's torque. Mc'Corkle
rises from floor, embarrassed.

                         MC'CORKLE
               Looks like Borgnine is doing some
               real damage on Marvin.

ON TV - EARNEST BORGNINE whacks Marvin with chain.

                         SKINNER
               Neither. They ain't true bums.

                         MC'CORKLE
               Where we going?

                         JASPER
               Nine-O-five rollin' to Sac, then
               Reno. Ol' Skinny here needs
               medical attention.

Skinner flexes arm, simulates playing slot machine.

                         SKINNER
               I need the exercise.

INT. 917 KUMQUAT JUICE BOXCAR - NIGHT

TRIO, FRANK, HARRY in lavish boxcar, western decor.
Fireplace lit. Solid metal door open. Sliding glass door
allows a view. They watch big screen TV, "Emperor of the
North" movie.

ON TV - MARVIN whacks BORGNINE with hatchet.

DONNY soaks feet in steaming water, towel wrapped around
head, water SLOSHES gently from train movement. The CLICKITY-
CLICK-CLACK of wheels sets the tone.

                         DICK
                    (to Cliff, loudly)
              Hey, this is the good life, huh?

Cliff's eyes locked on TV, chomps popcorn. Lee Marvin
talking to Cigarette on TV.

                         HARRY
              Shhh! The kid ain't gonna make it.

ON TV - MARVIN throws CIGARETTE off train.

                         LEE MARVIN (V.O.)
                    (to Cigarette)
              Stay off the tracks. It's a bum's
              world for the bums.

EXT. ODYSSEY RESTAURANT / SAN FERNANDO VALLEY - NIGHT

YVONNE, CHRISTINE, DEBBIE sit by outdoor firepit, sip
Margaritas. Highway-405 car lights resemble rubies and
diamonds snaking through valley floor slithering up distant
hills. Streetlights and stars glitter.

                         YVONNE
              Mc'Corkle didn't call back.

                         DEBBIE
              So? He's busy chasing those bums.

                         YVONNE
              His phone is disconnected. I
              think he defected.

                         CHRISTINE
              C'mon, now your getting paranoid.

Yvonne searches pocketbook.

                         YVONNE
              I am not. Something is going on.

Whatever she's looking for she can't find. She places hand
down blouse, arm deep into cleavage. TWO MEN above stare.
Yvonne pulls out a magazine, turns pages, hands it to
Christine.
                         CHRISTINE
              Nooo! You all must be joking?

                         YVONNE
              Yeeess! Moonlight and roses.

                         DEBBIE
                    (eyes bulging)
              That little rat!

Debbie grabs magazine, tries to tear it, but she can't. She
rises, flings it to fire. Magazine page -"Why Successful Men
Ride the Iron Road". PHOTO - Bikinied sweeties pose on diesel
locomotive engine. Six well-dressed men stand in f.g.

                    YVONNE
          It's time we kick some bums!

INT. YVONNE'S LIVING ROOM - DAY

YVONNE, DEBBIE, CHRISTINE watch TV as they pack clothes.

EXT. APARTMENT COMPLEX / VAN NUYS - DAY

KAREN SIREN (29) and DARLENE FRIZZY (21) lounge by pool,
watch portable TV revealing commercials. They flip pages
from a stack of, "LA's Wealthy Eligible Bachelor" magazines.

ROGER MOOTOO (20) and TOM STEWEY (21) spy from balcony.
Roger hands Tom a magazine cover, photo of themselves
imprinted on, "LA's Wealthy Eligible Bachelor" magazine.

TV on balcony tuned to same channel the girls watch.

                    ROGER
          I can't believe it, Tom. We tried
          it and still didn't work.

                    TOM
          We're dealing with Valley Girl
          mentality, dude. We need to do
          something more simplistic like buy
          a Mercedes.

                    ROGER
          Oh, simple, huh? We can't afford
          sixty-grand never mind put gas in
          the blasted thing.

ON TV - "Travel with the Rich" show.

                    TOM
          Shhh! Show is starting.

On TV - HOST with British dialect over a montage of exotic
locations of the world.

                    HOST (V.O.)
          Welcome to Travel with the Rich.
          This week we reveal the secret
          getaway of wealthy men.

          Looking for Mr. Right with money
          and brights? Take flight to the
          iron highway.

On TV - Dirty SD-40's pulling boxcars. Horn blows. ENGINEER
waves. HOBOES hang on boxcar ladders, some sit on flatcars
play cards, throw dice.

Valley girls and dudes eyes glued to TV sets.

                    HOST (V.O.)
                    (continuing)
          A perfect hide for the rich man.
          No one would have dreamed that the
          hoboes you see may be
          multimillionaires escaping the
          crowds and confusion of the city.
          Truly a secret society of the
          wealthy. Punch your ticket and
          stay with us as we ride the rails
          of gold to the annual Sacramento
          Rail Day Celebration.

ELISE and CHARLOTTE introduced on TV.

                    HOST (V.O.)
                    (continuing)
          What advice can you tell a young
          gold digger?

                    ELISE (V.O.)
          There's gold on them thar rails.
          Nuggets of untold wealth ripe for
          the pickin's for those who dare to
          prospect.

Microphone swings to Charlotte as pusher engines THUNDER by
in b.g. ENGINEER and FIREMAN wave, HORN blows. TRIO, FRANK
and HARRY smile and wave from boxcar. DONNY almost falls
out, they catch him.

INT. YVONNE'S LIVING ROOM - DAY

CHRISTINE sees DONNY on TV. She SCREAMS. YVONNE and DEBBIE
also SCREAM seeing DICK and CLIFF. They kick TV until it
EXPLODES.

BACK TO SCENE / ON TV

                    CHARLOTTE (V.O.)
          I've always wondered where rich
          men go. I searched night clubs,
          golf courses, marinas.
          Sure, you see a few, most are
          spoken for, but it's right here on
          the railroad where eligible men of
          influence spend most of their time.

EXT. R.R. TRACKS BY UNIVERSE STUDIOS - DAY

YVONNE, CHRISTINE, DEBBIE in skirts, stand by tracks and a
pile of suitcases ten-feet tall. ELISE and CHARLOTTE present.

                    CHARLOTTE
               (disgusted)
          Ladies don't hump trains.

                    YVONNE
          It's the principle. He vowed for
          better or for worse, till death do
          us part.

Christine and Debbie nod. A weak train horn TOOTS! Rickety
small Alco SWITCHER engine approaches.

                    ELISE
          They don't hear the worse.

Christine sharpens fingernails with file.

                    CHRISTINE
          Donny's going to remember the
          death part when I get my nails
          into his skull.

Engine's bell closer DING! DING! DING!

                    YVONNE
          Humiliation, abandonment, disgrace
          and poverty that's what it's all
          about. They have denied us the
          dignity and satisfaction of seeing
          them squirm in divorce court.

INT. CAB OF SWITCHER - DAY

ENGINEER POV - WIVES hitchhike. Train slows. Brakes SQUEAK.

                    ENGINEER
               (to Fireman)
          I don't think the bums are gonna
          like this. Not one bit.

                    FIREMAN
          Ya'gotta stop, Fred. Sexual
          discrimination laws. You know
          what happened to old Fly Ash.

                    ENGINEER
          This is going to create problems,
          Pookie. Big problems. I mean it.

FRED slides lever, air brakes activate PSSST! Engine
SHUTTERS, RATTLES, SQUEAKS, backfires KA-POW! Engine stops.

BACK TO SCENE

Rickety old rusted switcher skids to stop. Engine pulls
flatcar with crane and shovel. WIVES hug, sob good-byes.

POOKIE operates crane's shovel, teeth grasps, punctures
luggage, lifts to flatcar. Drops luggage, contents spill.

Pookie, embarrassed, sees women's underwear. Blast of
compressed air raises ladies skirts PSSST! They SCREAM.

FRED and Pookie assist wives to board engine, step inside
cab, horn blows TOOT! TOOT! Wives stand on engine platform
wave hankies as train leaves, in reverse PUTT! PUTT! PUTT!
Puffing smoke, CLANKING, the little engine has no guts.

Train accelerates, wind blows ladies underwear by cab
windows. Fred reaches out, catches a bra.

                    FRED
          Pookie, this is gonna cause
          trouble.

Train stops. Pookie throws switch. Train moves forward.

EXT. BY R.R.TRACKS - DAY

                    CHARLOTTE
          Are they doing the right thing?

                    ELISE
          A woman can do no wrong. Two can
          do better. Three will see
          perfection. I think they're nuts!

                    CHARLOTTE
          I thought you said a woman has to
          go after the man she loves?

                    ELISE
          Absolutely, but these gals want to
          love their husbands to death.

INT. 917 KUMQUAT JUICE BOXCAR - MORNING

TRIO naps on floor. Room is a mess. DONNY'S face in bowl of
Jell-O, toes down in bucket of water. FRANK and HARRY
strapped to the wall like two astronauts, SNORING, pillows
tucked between head and wall.

Train decelerates to a full stop. Door slides open.

                    MC'CORKLE
          Get up you bunch of bums.

MC'CORKLE smiles, reveals rotten teeth. Everyone awakens.
Frank and Harry unstrap.

Outside - a field of flowers cluttered with toilet bowls
glistening in the morning sunrise as far as the eye can see.

                    DICK
          Get a load of this. I never in my
          life saw the likes of it.

                    DONNY
          Must be a rest stop.

DICK, frowns at the sight. Jumps out of boxcar. CLIFF jumps
too. Donny looks down, freezes.

                    CLIFF
          C'mon, Donny. You can do it.

Donny sits on edge of floor, cautiously slides out. Frank
and Harry dumbfounded, shake their heads. Frank pushes a
button by the door, stairs unfold. They step outside. Trio
and Mc'Corkle embarrassed. Frank points to the field of
toilet bowls.

                    FRANK
                 (to Dick)
          This is their final resting place.

Dick is amazed. Mc'Corkle smiles, exposes his rotten teeth
to Harry. Harry gets right in his face.

                    HARRY
          Take the rot out of that smile.

Mc'Corkle's smile dissolves. Frank quickly jams his arm
between them.

                    FRANK
                 (to Harry)
          He's a postulant, he doesn't know.
          I'll take care of it.

                    HARRY
          I don't like it, Frank. Deal with
          it.

Harry stomps to engine. Frank pulls Mc'Corkle by arm into
the field of toilet bowls. They sit on commodes, face each
other. Frank scolds him MOS. Mc'Corkle picks, spits wax
from teeth.

Frank walks to Trio. Mc'Corkle in b.g. sits like the
thinking man on a bowl.

                    DICK
          I don't get it, Frank. What's
          pulling Harry's chain?

                              FRANK
                    Even a true bum doesn't want to be
                    a bum.

INT. SWITCHER / VENTURA - MORNING

CHILDREN on trestle wave hands. Engine SPUTTERS, CLANKS,
cylinders misfire POW! Pitiful horn TOOT! FRED and POOKIE do
not wave, but WIVES do. Car HORNS blow, hands in cars wave.

EXT. SWITCHER / RINCON - DAY

Engine heads north by ocean. Motorhomes line roadside,
TOURISTS wave. Engine horn blows TOOT! TOOT! Only the WIVES
wave.

INT. SWITCHER - DAY

YVONNE in engineer seat, waves to RV campers.

                              YVONNE
                         (to Pookie)
                    I tell you those crumb-bums are
                    going to pay.

POOKIE in fireman's seat. FRED, CHRISTINE, DEBBIE stand,
hold hands as train rocks.

                              POOKIE
                         (to Yvonne)
                    Many husbands run out on their
                    wives. Cut engine speed one notch.

Yvonne snaps throttle lever to #2 notch. Everyone loses
balance.

                              FRED
                    It's not your fault. Don't blame
                    yourself. A bum isn't worth
                    having.

                              CHRISTINE
                    Donny has such a cute bum. That's
                    why I married the bum.

                              DEBBIE
                    Pookie? Why do men have to be
                    bums?

PEOPLE ahead on rails step off track as engine approaches.
They wave. Yvonne pulls lanyard, TOOT! TOOT! KID throws a
tomato, splatters on side window. Everyone flinches.

                              POOKIE
                    We work for the railroad.

                         DEBBIE
              I mean, want to be bums.

Pookie takes Debbie by the hand.

                         POOKIE
              Sweetheart, there are good bums
              and bad bums and twenty different
              subspecies of bums within the two
              categories. Your bum will be a
              better bum, if you let him be a
              bum.

Wives gawk to each other, absorb words of wisdom.

                         YVONNE
              He means there are three types of
              men. Lovers, thrill-seekers, but
              the happiest are imbeciles.

                         CHRISTINE
              Marriage is the supreme blunder
              all women make.

INT. KUMQUAT JUICE BOXCAR / MOUNTAINS - DAY

                         FRANK
                    (to Dick)
              Every woman should marry, but no
              man.

EXT. R.R. TRACKS BY BEACH - DAY

Switcher ascends mountain pass. Underwear from ruptured
luggage litter tracks. CHILDREN hold them high on twigs.
Embarrassed MOTHERS chase and retrieve underwear.

INT. SWITCHER - DAY

Switcher passes R.R. crossing. Arms drop, red lights flash,
DING! DING! DING! Engine enters freight yard, stops by depot.

                         FRED
              End of the line. She's all yours.
              Follow the green signal lights,
              stay on track number-one and
              you'll be in Sacramento in no time.

WIVES nervous. POOKIE points to tracks dead straight ahead.

                          POOKIE
          Nothing too it. Remember, if you
          see a yellow vehicle don't wave to
          him. That's the Trainmaster, ol'
          Iron Face. His job to discipline
          trespassers on the line. He'll be
          looking for you when he discovers
          his little mule missing.
                    (beat)
          You can always tell a bum from a
          real engineer. A true bum will
          always wave back if you wave to
          him. It's the secret signal. I
          can tell you no more.

Wives kiss Fred and Pookie on cheek. Debbie affectionately
pinches Pookie's left cheek.

                          DEBBIE
          It's called a five-year itch? I
          promise you, Pookie, I will give
          Clifford the five-year bitch
          before the new moon rises.

Fred and Pookie disembark. Yvonne inches throttle, switcher
comes to life slowly creeping by a yellow vehicle.

TRAINMASTER- IRON FACE (60) inside the vehicle reads
schedules, doesn't lift eyes from page. Hand from switcher
cab waves. Another hand grabs the waving hand, pulls it
inside cab.

Iron Face waves to switcher. No response.

EXT. LOS ANGELES RAIL YARD - DAY

KAREN and DARLENE wear tight blue jeans, high heels,
awkwardly trip on rail ties along track.

                          DARLENE
          Karen, there has got to be a
          better way to snag a rich man.

                          KAREN
          The odds are in our favor,
          Darlene. You don't see competition
          do you?

                          DARLENE
          I don't see any rich men.

They see two ragged HOBOES crossing the tracks.

                          KAREN AND DARLENE
          Now we do!

Red Mercedes convertible with auxiliary flanged wheels races
by on adjacent track. Two HOBOES in front seat, ROGER and
TOM. Banana peel sails, lands on Darlene's ankle. Lic.
plate,"T-Bums."

EXT. MOUNTAINS - DAY

ENGINEER POV - Looks alongside boiler of a steam locomotive
racing through a forest. Billows of black smoke pour from
smoke stack. Crosses over a wood trestle by a waterfall,
river below.

Diesel locomotive comes on from inside mountain tunnel,
WHISTLES and HORNS blow. CRASH! PSSSSS! Cloud of steam.

WIDER VIEW - Twisted train wreckage, smoking metal scattered
along tunnel entrance.

                    BILL'S VOICE (V.O.)
          Are you okay?

WIDER VIEW - Model railroad set and two men behind
sophisticated controls. TV monitors mounted into console.
TV monitor reveals wreckage. Each wears Casey Jones style
hats.

                    BILL
          Norman, you need to switch to
          track number one on the Donner
          Pass grade otherwise you enter the
          "Big Hole" heading West.

                    NORMAN
          Bill, the grade is too steep for
          steam locomotives at that speed.
          Water primed the cylinder, blew
          the head clear off. I lost steam
          pressure and air brake control. It
          can't be done, Bill. Track is
          designed for diesels.

Bill removes small camera from wrecked locomotive.

                    BILL
          Never say never. Let's try it
          again, but this time lower the
          water to one gage, shut off the
          injector and trim the throttle to
          raise superheat temperature.

Fire leaps from under steam locomotive. Bill and Norman grab
CO_2 fire extinguishers, snuff flames.

                    NORMAN
          I haven't spent all my money yet,
          and I don't want to die for a
          cheap thrill.

                         BILL
            Think of the glory not the gory.

FOOTSTEPS above, door CREAKS open o.s.

                    WOMAN'S VOICE (V.O.)
            Bill? What's going on? You okay?

                         BILL
                      (grumbling)
            Yes, sweetie.

EXT. 917 / MOUNTAIN TERRAIN - DAY

917 rumbles a canyon curve along whitewater rapids. Engines
heavily pound the air, blowers cry with sad whines, heavy
black smoke flow from vents as it strains steep grade. Wheel
flanges spark and SQUEAL.

Engines tower upon us as they thunder by, leave us in a haze
of swirling diesel exhaust. Box cars CREAK and MOAN as they
glide by CLUNK! CLUNK!   CLUNK! CLUNK!

INT. KUMQUAT JUICE BOXCAR - DAY

DICK and CLIFF smile, talk MOS, sit by doorway, dangle feet
in air. DONNY cautiously stands inside, holds a mirror out
doorway, gazes into mirror.

INT. 917 ENGINE CAB - DAY

                         CASEY
                      (to fireman)
            Sparky? Have you ever thought of?
            You know?

                         SPARKY
            Have you?

                         CASEY
            Takes courage to cross that line.
            You got to respect that.

                         SPARKY
            I have no regrets, Casey.

BUM standing by track frantically waving. Casey and Sparky
don't see him.

                         CASEY
            Contemplating the what-if's. I
            just think. What the hell am I
            saying?

Signal bridge light flashes red. Black and yellow metal flag
rises, Casey and Sparky don't notice it.

                              SPARKY
                    You're serious?

                              CASEY
                    I mean life would be different,
                    maybe fun. Know what I mean?

Railroad WORKER ahead crouched over a rail, looks up, runs
for his life, YELLS into walkie-talkie. Casey and Sparky
chattering don't see him. Another WORKER rubs palms of hands
together warning train to stop. He runs off track.

                              SPARKY
                    The grass always looks greener on
                    the other side but when you get
                    there it ain't so green. Anyway,
                    you took a vow so there ain't no
                    lookin' back. You're talkin' big
                    again. You ain't strong enough to
                    face the real world and you know
                    it.

917 screeches around curve. On straight tracts; Three two-
inch square red patches on the rail. Casey and Sparky not
paying attention. BOOM! BOOM! BOOM!

                              SPARKY
                         (continuing; panic)
                    Torpedoes!

Casey slams throttle, train lurches, a violent deceleration.
Couplings compress KA-BOOM! They're thrown forwards in their
seats. Sparky grabs lanyard, blows HORN repeatedly.

Casey flips emergency brake switch. Console flashes red
warning lights. Alarms BUZZ and PING.

Casey notches dynamic braking lever, needle on brake scale
doesn't budge. See WORK CREW scatter off the rails. Red
fusee's burn beside rails.

Sparky runs along platform, enters smoke-filled generator
room. Blue bolt of electricity leaps from generator, passes
right by Sparky's face ZAP! Singes his hair into small curls.

He runs back to Casey, yells through window over the RUMBLE
and WHINE of engines.

                              SPARKY
                         (continuing)
                    Number one meltdown. Kill it!

Casey opens 600 volt cabinet, pulls main disconnect. Console
lights fade. Sound of the big engines die. Only the SINGING
wheels scouring steel rails and the SQUEAL of brake pads is
heard.

Train rolls to equipment parked on the rails. Work crew jump
inside vehicles, speed away in panic. Three red torpedoes
approach, and a large red object rises up from the rail.

                    SPARKY
                 (continuing)
            Derailer, we got to go.

Locomotive squishes torpedoes BOOM! BOOM! BOOM! Casey and
Sparky leap and tumble out of sight.

INTERCUT - INT. KUMQUAT JUICE BOXCAR - DAY

Everyone panic-stricken except FRANK and HARRY stand by door
looking along the boxcars, see engines smash equipment on
rails. White clouds of smoke swirl from all wheels.

They look down, see SCREECHING wheels glowing red, showers of
blue/green sparks with a mix of gold from brake shoes.

                    FRANK
            I thought I heard it the first
            time. Time to say good-bye.
            Harry, get the gear.

Harry pulls suitcase from under couch, tosses to CLIFF in
fire brigade manner to DONNY, DICK, MC'CORKLE, then Frank.
Frank opens case, gives everyone a wide belt with ten-foot
nylon string, with hook on end.

                    HARRY
            Put it on. Buckle it tight.

They strap on belts, step to doorway.

                    FRANK
            Hook up.

They attach string clasp to eyebolts above door, hold hands.
Looking up tracks, they see lead locomotive derail and kick
up gravel. Like dominoes, each engine and boxcar falls in
turn KA- BOOM! KA-BOOM! KA-BOOM! Train decelerates with
tremendous force.

                    FRANK
                 (continuing)
            When I say jump. Ready?

Ten boxcars topple over. Frank counts.

                    FRANK
                 (continuing)
            Six, five, four, three, two, jump!

Frank leaps, others follow, Harry last. Ripcords catch,
release a valve on each belt as they leap in midair PSSST!
Boxcar now tips over.

Huge balloons inflate from the belts engulfing each of them into a multicolored ball. The balloons bounce along the ground like basketballs splashing in river below.

They float into rapids, tumble over waterfall. A balloon bounces off Dick's balloon.

                    DICK'S VOICE (V.O.)
          Don't burst my bubble.

SERIES OF SHOTS / VARIOUS LOCATIONS - DAY

MUSIC score similar to, "Tom Sawyer" by Rush group.

- - Switcher approaches banner over tracks, "Welcome to Sacramento. Ten Easy Miles Ahead." WIVES wave.

- - Angry WOMEN holding heavy 3/8" chains board a pink AMTAK train in San Francisco powered by two E9's. TV REPORTER on scene.

                    REPORTER
          A mad rush to Sacramento. These
          gals are destined to chain up
          their bums to bring them to
          justice. Lawyers, doctors, men of
          prestigious professions have
          humped the trains. Never have we
          witnessed such a mass exodus since
          the gold rush of eighteen-forty-
          nine.

- - Six windblown bearded faces, hair slicked in the wind, arms high over heads. Heavy throated note of Harley Davidson engines.

WIDER VIEW - BUMS ride choppers on the rails. Special rigging grips wheels to track.

- - WIVES drive switcher in center of street, disrupts traffic. Crane swings free, smashes cars. Wives ask directions from angry drivers. COP (30) chases on foot, but gives up when switcher enters a tunnel.

- - Freight train climbs a serpentine grade in Cajon Pass.

- - BUMS seat themselves inside a 727 jet.

- - BUMS inside a new car, scenery rolls by side windows.

- - Scenery passes by windows of 727 jet.

WIDER VIEW - Car is on a train's flatcar. So is the fuselage of the 727 airplane with no wings. BUMS wave through windows.

- - Two HOBOES gold pan on American river see the six balloons float by. They exchange looks, each swigs whisky.

- - Freight train winds through Tehachapi Loop. Bums stand on
boxcars, dive into water-filled hoppercar swimming pools.
Others suntan on empty flatcars.

- -Two trains drag race side-by-side through Cajon Pass.
Train HOBBYISTS cheer as trains exit curve. Two MEN bravely
stand between trains, SCREAMING.

- - NORMAN and BILL dressed in rags stand on boxcar ladder as
train pulls into Old Town, Sacramento behind California State
Railroad Museum. They jump off, grin as they gaze at museum.

- - Six balloons float by Old Town on Sacramento River.
TRIO, MC'CORKLE, FRANK, HARRY'S heads poke from balloons.
BUMS behind museum toss ropes, they catch with their teeth,
pulled to shore.

MUSIC fades.

- - switcher arrives at siding behind railroad museum.
YVONNE, CHRISTINE, DEBBIE scan area with binoculars.
Husbands out of view on river embankment. Wives stumble as
they walk to Old Town.

- - AMTAK train arrives. Upset WOMEN with 3/8" chains rush
off train double-time. Ankles twist as they awkwardly
stumble in high heels on track gravel.

EXT. OLD TOWN SACRAMENTO - DAY

Red, white and blue banners lace Main Street. Light poles,
buildings dressed with flags. Parade - Antique fire engines,
steam engines, floats depict gold rush era, old PROSPECTORS
on floats wave to crowd. MUSICAL BAND of BUMS march forward.

On sidewalks, BUMS mixed with TOURIST. Bums nervous, look
over shoulders, shifty-eyes, walk cautiously. BILL and
NORMAN duck into Hastings Building as two angry LADIES
approach.

As ladies pass, BILL and NORMAN'S eyes peek at them with
relieved expressions. They walk down sidewalk, enter a
recessed entry. TRIO, FRANK, HARRY, MC'CORKLE follow, sneak
upstairs.

Float passes by, puffing steam locomotive with Engineer and
Fireman wave to crowd, toss candy to CHILDREN. DOG competes
for candy. Children shoo it away, but dog flashes teeth, kids
run, dog resumes eating the candy.

YVONNE, CHRISTINE, DEBBIE pass by entry, stop, continue
walking with expressions of undercover spies diligently
scanning crowd.

MAN with dog walks by a WINO with hand extended.

                        WINO
              Say, pal, I haven't had a bite in
              days.

                        MAN
              Oh, yeah? I'll give ya a bite.
              Get him, pooch!

Dog leaps, bites wino's shoe, YEOW!

EXT. RESTAURANT / UPPER BALCONY - DAY

Reservation cards on table. BILL and NORMAN sit at table.
TRIO, FRANK, HARRY, MC'CORKLE stumble in.

                        BILL
              Frank, good to see you could make
              it. Harry, your looking crabby as
              usual. Who are they?

Frank introduces everyone. WAITER dressed as a gold miner
brings bottles of whisky, bowl of flaming red Jell-O and
fortune cookies.

                        NORMAN
              Anybody follow you?

                        HARRY
              One of these day's I'm going to
              sue you.

                        FRANK
              Not in my court. Now look guys,
              this is the plan.

INT. RESTAURANT LOBBY - DAY

DICK reads electronic ticker tape sign over a restroom
doorway, "Air Quality Unhealthy. Stage 2 Ozone Health
Hazard."

INT. MEN'S RESTROOM - DAY

Dick's face distorts, pinches nose. MEN HOWL and GASP from
stalls. Sound of gasses released PFFFFT!

                        MEN IN STALLS (V.O.)
                          (randomly)
              "Ow! Blasted hemorrhoids are
              killing me. Somebody help me!"
              "C'mon sweetheart be nice to me.
              Ow! Ow!" "Oh, no. I got the
              flue." "Who peed on the toilet
              seat?" "I did, heh-heh-heh!"

Dick steps to urinal. Wet mop pushed over shoes. Dick sees
PORTER wears gas mask.

                         WOMAN'S VOICE (V.O.)
                          (terrified scream)
                 Let go of me. Help! Help! Get
                 your filthy hands off of me you
                 perverted pig. Help!

Dick spins, looks to stalls. Men come and go as if nothing
is wrong. Dick approaches a stall, BANGS on door with fist.

                              DICK
                 You okay? What's going on?

                         WOMAN'S VOICE (V.O.)
                 Somebody help me. Oh, please help
                 me!

Sound of clothes TEAR and a woman SCREAMS o.s.

INT. RESTROOM STALL - DAY

MAN sits on commode with wide-eyes, sees DICK'S shoes by the
door. Door jolts as Dick pounds it.

                           MAN IN STALL
                 I'll be done in a minute.

                         WOMAN'S VOICE (V.O.)
                 Help. He's raping me. Somebody
                 please help me!

EXT. RESTROOM STALL - DAY

DICK furiously grabs top of door, yanks hard, breaks it away.
MAN looks up at Dick, jaw drops, whips out a badge.

                         MAN'S VOICE (V.O.)
                 Police. You're under arrest.
                 Breaking and entering, soliciting
                 sex in public restroom, disturbing
                 the peace. Freeze!

Dick throws door on the man, runs out of stall area. Up on
wall - TV set reveals a woman wrapped in a towel standing
behind cops who cuff up a man. Dick doesn't see the TV.

EXT. R.R.TRACKS / BEHIND RAILROAD MUSEUM - DAY

Red Mercedes slows to a stop. It's ROGER and TOM. They park
on a siding by idling SD-40 engines. Step out of car dressed
in filthy, torn-to-shreds clothes. #905 train arrives.

EXT. 905 FREIGHT TRAIN / SUGAR BEET EXPRESS BOXCAR - DAY

Door slides open. It's KAREN and DARLENE. They look like a
million bucks. Shimmy out of doorway onto ground, see red
Mercedes with "T-Bums" lic. plate. TOM and ROGER walk to town.

                        KAREN
              Wiggle the bait, Darlene. These
              bums like bums.

Silver Rolls Royce pulls to siding. License tag, "Rich-Bum."
It's rigged with auxiliary flange wheels. MR. SIMMONS steps
out, dressed in rags, walks fast to town, blends with
TOURISTS.

Valley Girls follow, high-heels twist ankles in gravel. They
lose sight of bums.

                        DARLENE
              We'll never get a rich man if they
              keep running away from us.

Karen and Darlene walk past a tankcar, see a seedy HOBO
leaning against wheel, SNORES, drools, tongue on cheek.
Whisky bottle in crotch. They stare, flies on his face.

                        KAREN
              He's worth, millions!

EXT. STOREFRONT UPPER BALCONY - DAY

LOUD commotion in street below. BILL, NORMAN, TRIO,
MC'CORKLE, FRANK, HARRY rise from seats, peek over balcony,
eyebrows reach the sky.

EXT. STREET BELOW - DAY

WOMEN grab BUMS, yank them from all different parts of their
bodies, drag them away. The bums resist to no avail.

                        BUMS
                    (randomly)
              "Please, honey. Let me stay."   "I
              promise I won't do it again."
              "Honestly, I took a wrong turn on
              freeway." "I don't wanna go home."

BACK TO SCENE

                        HARRY
              Many are called, few are chosen.
              Those poor souls are going home.

DICK, DONNY, CLIFF alarmed. Donny bites fingernails,
eyebrows fluctuate up and down.

                        FRANK
              Happens every year. I hate to
              think how miserable those poor
              bums lives will be now.

Bill peeks over banister. GP-60M's arrive in b.g.

                BILL
        Hey, look at them boomers!

Everyone peers over banister, see YVONNE, CHRISTINE, DEBBIE
pass flyers. Dick, Donny and Cliff recoil, hug the floor.

                BILL
          (continuing)
        Not the women, stupid. The
        engines. GP Sixty-M's.

                DICK
        That's our wives! How did they
        find us?

EXT. SUTTER FORT - DAY

Two BUMS by an old muzzle-loader cannon.

              FIRST BUM
        Are you sure?

             SECOND BUM
        Women. Trainloads. It's an
        invasion.

BACK TO SCENE

MC'CORKLE steps from banister, pretends he doesn't know
wives, shrugs shoulders. DONNY rubs scalp, sweat pours from
his face.

CLIFF'S fingers grasp lower teeth, shivers with fear, stares
like a zombie at Donny who acts the same.

               CLIFF
        She's gonna catch me. She's gonna
        catch me. I shouldn't have done
        it. I can't face her and live.
        I got to get out of here.

DICK'S grim-face beams hard at Mc'Corkle. Mc'Corkle struggles
to hold his composure.

               DICK
        So, they want to play games? I
        can play too. No one will
        humiliates me like this and gets
        away with it. A man has a right
        to live as he pleases.

Cliff opens a fortune cookie, "Go home! Lest sinister
circumstance befall thee." Throws cookie over banister,
lands on Yvonne's head. She looks up. Sees a pigeon's tail on
roof ledge.

                    YVONNE
          They even have the birds trained!

EXT. SUTTER FORT - DAY

Two BUMS light fuse on canon and run.

BACK TO SCENE

MC'CORKLE'S relieved. TRIO sniveling. KAREN and DARLENE
enter, sit at next table, cross legs, divulge flirting eyes.
Everyone disregards them. Sound of the cannon BOOM! o.s.

                    FRANK
               (terror in eyes)
          The warning signal.

                    HARRY
          A little too late is always too
          late.

EXT. SIDEWALK BELOW - DAY

YVONNE, CHRISTINE, DEBBIE under balcony glance up, then gaze
to entry. Debbie enters, exits with a BUM, reads flyer, wags
his head, walks away. Flyer - picture of Dick, Donny and
Cliff, "Wanted Bruised or Abused $10,000 Reward."

Wives pass flyers to PEOPLE on sidewalk as parade marches by.
BUMS avoid them. Three MEN we saw earlier boarding a freight
train dressed in business suits study the flyers, point down
the street. Wives leave. The men follow.

ROGER and TOM pass by them on sidewalk. Debbie grabs Roger
by the throat, looks at him hard, then lets him go. Roger
rubs his throat as he backs away.

                    DEBBIE
          You're lucky I don't love you!

EXT. SIDE STREET / OLD SACRAMENTO - DAY

DICK'S dirty brown shoes below a store front window. Shoes
SQUISH as they approach door, a JINGLE of bells as door
swings open. Door closes with a JINGLE. Squishy shoes
approach counter.

                    WOMAN AT COUNTER
          Quality meets your expectations?

Dick's hand exchanges credit card with WOMAN, then folds
NEWSPAPER under arm. Door SLAMS, bells JINGLE. Woman with
puzzled expression. We never see Dick's face.

EXT. OLD TOWN SACRAMENTO - NIGHT

Gaslights flicker soft hues against dim storefront windows.
Sidewalks empty. A few straggling BUMS stroll to R.R.
tracks. COP (30) walks beat, swings nightstick. Train HORN
echoes o.s.

HARRY stands at ATM machine. Head down, hands by crotch. A
sign, "NIGHT DEPOSIT." He GROANS, GASPS, legs wobble,
relaxes, breathes a sigh of relief. ZIPS fly, takes money,
steps aside, reveals a sign, "SPERM BANK."

EXT. ACROSS THE STREET - NIGHT

KAREN and DARLENE marvel at JEWELRY STORE window, point at
heavy gauge gold chains and padlocks.

                    DARLENE
          The bum I marry will look
          respectable in that one. Case
          hardened steel too!

They stop by THE BRIDES DREAM store. Two MANNEQUINS chained
together at waist. GROOM mannequin - horror on his face,
stares at chain in hand. BRIDE - all smiles.

INT. SWITCHER - NIGHT

WIVES inside cab scan NEWSPAPER, flip pages frantically.
Steaming tea cups on engine console.

                    YVONNE
          My gosh, that's my home!

ON NEWSPAPER - front page, photo of hillside homes in flames.
Headlines, "Raging Firestorm Incinerates Pacific Palisades."

CHRISTINE snatches telephone, dials eleven digits.

                    CHRISTINE
          How bad is that fire?

SPLIT SCREEN / CHRISTINE AND MAID.

MAID sprays fire extinguisher into smoking oven.

                    MAID
              (on phone)
          It's not bad, house is a bit
          smoky. Nothing to worry about,
          really. When you coming home?

Yvonne grabs phone, hands shake, full panic.

                    YVONNE
          This is Yvonne, is my house okay?

                        MAID
             I don't know, I've been battling
             my own blazes. How did you know
             about the fire?

                        YVONNE
             It's in the bloody newspapers!

Maid's eyebrows compress to nose. They both hang up.

                        DEBBIE
             I guess we should go home now.

Yvonne and christine punch fist into palm.

                        CHRISTINE
             Not a chance. Payback's a bitch.

                        YVONNE
             When you're up to your neck in hot
             water, be like a teapot and sing.
                    (beat)
             We have insurance.

They SING, clap hands.

                        WIVES
                    (singing)
             Were gonna catch those crumb-bums,
             spank some butt. Those good-for-
             nothin' husbands. Rah! Rah! Kick
             their bum's to kingdom come.

They kick, laugh, hug, toast, sip tea.

EXT. BEHIND RAILROAD MUSEUM - NIGHT

TRIO, MC'CORKLE, FRANK, HARRY, BILL, NORMAN creep to side
door. They KNOCK. Door opens, SECURITY GUARD lets them in.

INT. RAILROAD MUSEUM - NIGHT

Their eyes glaze over, jaws limp.

                        DICK
             It's beautiful.

Spit-polished vintage Baldwin steam locomotive #001 sits
silently under glow of lights. Coal and watercar coupled.
Bill and Norman get right to work, climb aboard the cab.

                        BILL
             Matthias William Baldwin's
             personal locomotive, built in
             1851. It's got the power of six
             modern diesels. C'mon, there's
             work to do.

Frank restrains Harry by arm.

                    FRANK
          They need to take their vows.

All place hands over their hearts and repeat Harry's dialog
with solemn sacredness.

                    HARRY
          I solemnly pledge. To protect and
          honor my brother bum. And never
          tell his wife no matter how good
          looking she is or what she may
          offer me for information which may
          lead to his capture. With all my
          heart I promise to be a good bum.
          Amen.

                    FRANK
          You are now, true bums.

Harry pins a small silver medallion on their shirts, "TB."
They rejoice and get to work on locomotive. Mc'Corkle fondles
medallion, takes a breath, appears perplexed.

BACK TO SCENE

COP with nightstick tries doorknob. It turns. He cautiously
enters. SECURITY GUARD approaches him.

                    COP
          Can I see the train again?

                    SECURITY GUARD
                 (British accent)
          We're really busy tonight. I
          thought the door was locked?

                    COP
          What's that smell? Smells like
          coal burning.

                    SECURITY GUARD
          Ma gosh, my dinner is burnin'.
          Look, come back tomorrow night
          okay? Cheers 'ol chap.

                    COP
                 (whimpers, pouts)
          But I want to see the train.

Guard escorts cop to door. Steam whistle TOOT!

                    COP
                 (continuing)
          Hey, what's going on here?

Cop hits guard with club on head CLUNK! Hat flips off, metal
pot on head. Guard punches cop in stomach OUCH! Kicks him in
butt and out the door he goes landing on sidewalk.

EXT. SIDEWALK BY RAILROAD MUSEUM ENTRY - NIGHT

COP leaps up, door slams in his face. He bangs door with
stick, HOLLERS. Kicks and rams door.

BACK TO SCENE

GUARD scurries to steam locomotive.

                    GUARD
          Hurry up! Cops comin'.

Men work a frenzied pace stoking boiler furnace, black smoke
pours from smokestack, steam HISSES along cylinder drips.
Frank's soaked head pops from top lid of watercar.

                    FRANK
          I'm ready. How about you guys?

                    BILL
          It's now or never guys. All
          aboard!

INT. SWITCHER / CAB - SUNRISE

WIVES slouched, snooze in chairs. Underwear hangs from
engine control levers. DEBBIE cradles a stuffed raccoon in
arms. CHRISTINE has a pincushion voodoo doll on her lap
named, "Donald" with needle in his butt.

KA-BOOM! Baldwin smashes through rear door of museum, passes
switcher. Wives jolt to feet, see husbands tumble off-
balance on coalcar.

                    YVONNE
          Throttle up. It's time to play.

Christine hops to engineer's seat, releases air brake PSSST!
Notches throttle to #1 VROOM! VROOM! VROOM! Clicks throttle
to #3. Blowers WHINE, speed increases, but Baldwin has the
lead.

EXT. SWEET POTATO BOXCAR - NIGHT

KAREN and DARLENE in nighties watch trains leave.

                    DARLENE
          Karen, we have competition and
          they know how to drive trains.

                              KAREN
                    Frustrated rich bitches, Darlene.
                    That's what they are, but they
                    don't have what we got.

Karen wipes her hand along smooth contoured hips. BUMS run
down street to motorcycles, red Mercedes and silver Rolls
Royce on R.R. tracks, scramble into vehicles, accelerate down
the track.

COPS and WOMEN on foot slide to a stop by tracks. Cops wave
batons in air. They jog back up street out of view.

                              DARLENE
                    Will we ever catch a rich bum,
                    Karen? I want one sooo bad.

Darlene peeks over shoulder at her rear-end.

                              KAREN
                    Women have powers man can only
                    marvel at. Lets follow those
                    bewildered bums to the pot of gold
                    at the end of the line.

Karen peers at her breasts, then her shapely legs.

                              DARLENE
                    More powerful than a locomotive.

Giggling.

                              KAREN
                    Or a speeding bullet.

AMTAK train arrives. Horn blares staccato notes HONK! HONK!
Train stops, girls board train.

INT. SWITCHER - NIGHT

Baldwin blows black smoke into horizon well ahead of
switcher, throttle notched to #8 full-bore. Noise in cab -
CLUNKY, weak. Debbie grabs radio, hanky over mouthpiece.

                              DEBBIE
                         (scruffy voice)
                    Roseville, Mule One, status
                    please, over.

                              MALE VOICE (V.O.)
                    Mule One, traffic heavy. You're
                    clear to Roseville track one.

                              DEBBIE
                    Steamer, track two, unauthorized
                    transit. Milemarker one-eight-
                    four, over.

                          MALE VOICE (V.O.)
               Indicated. Trainmaster notified.
               Your clear, Mule One.

EXT. ROSEVILLE FREIGHT YARD - BREAK OF DAWN

R.R. EMPLOYEES stand on dispatch tower catwalk, scan distant
tracks with binoculars.

                          DISPATCHER
                     (shouts into radio)
               Visual contact track one. It's a,
               a Baldwin? Highballing!

Below tower, yellow utility trucks on track flash rotating
yellow lights. Railroad POLICE stand on tracks. IRON FACE
SCREAMS.

                          IRON FACE
                       (into radio)
                 Switch it! Switch it!

Dispatcher presses button. Track switch SLAMS into place.
BUM sits on switch, pinches his butt OUCH! Bum rips wire
from switch. Baldwin WHISTLE blows. Bum turns, sees Baldwin
bearing down. Leaps to feet, grabs switch lever, it's jammed.

He runs to next switch, but a R.R. COP stands by switchpost,
waves the bum to get off the road. Baldwin closes fast. Bum
steps behind cop, pees on cop's pants leg.

                          COP
               Hey, you dirty bum. I'll ring
               your --

Cop swings at bum, but he ducks, crouches low to ground. Bum
grabs cop's belt, pulls hard.

                          COP
                       (continuing)
               Let go, I'm a married man.

With foot above belt, bum flips cop over him. Runs to switch
in the nick of time, yanks lever, but it's locked. Cop
stands, dangles key in air, smiles. Bum's face turns white.

Baldwin POV - R.R. COPS scatter from vehicles. Cowcatcher
splits vehicles in two CRUNCH! Vehicles flip onto adjacent
tracks, one hits tower, knocks it over. MEN leap from
tilting tower, land on telephone cable, dangle above track
SCREAMING as Baldwin smokestack passes between their flailing
legs.

Freight trains on other tracks smack broken pieces of utility
trucks, shove them off the road. Baldwin exits yard, races
to Sierra foothills. Iron Face, in a full rage.

                         IRON FACE
                 The bums have got to go!

MOMENTS LATER

Roseville yard normalized. Men clear debris from tracks.
switcher rolls in at 20 m.p.h. Other locomotives busily
couple cars BOOM-BOOM! BOOM!

INT. SWITCHER - DAY

                         YVONNE
                 We need a faster engine, something
                 with class and a lot of power.

They pass by SWITCHMAN who gives a double-take look at the
WIVES waving at him. He waves, frowns, shakes head, walks
away, occasionally gawks over shoulder.

WORKMEN wash a set of ten brand spanking new SD-80
locomotives coupled to a beautiful black private car with
gold trimmings.
                         CHRISTINE
                 Hey, sugar. Check this out.

DEBBIE, CHRISTINE and YVONNE wink, slap hands.

EXT. ROSEVILLE YARD - DAY

Turn signal flashes on right side of switcher, pulls onto
siding.

WHISTLE blows, WORKMEN dump buckets, go to lunch. WIVES jog
to SD-80's, climb inside. CHRISTINE runs along platforms,
opens engine panels, turns the prime dial then switches it to
start. The big 16-cylinder engines ROAR to life, one-by-one.

INT. ROSEVILLE HEADQUARTERS - DAY

Three EXECUTIVES talk to MEDIA PERSONNEL.

                         FIRST EXECUTIVE
                           (childlike)
                 I've wanted a new train ever since
                 I was a kid. Now that I am
                 President of the Northern Sierra
                 Railroad, I got my train. Put
                 that in your magazine!

Reporters laugh, snap photo's of executives.

                         SECOND EXECUTIVE
                I'm sure you want to test ride our
                new engines. They'll be ready in
                a few minutes. You'll be highly impressed with
                the power. SD-80's have state of the art alternating
                electric current in these engines, not DC power.

SD-80's accelerate by the large picture window in b.g.
FEMALE REPORTER sees WIVES on engine platform, waving.

                         FEMALE REPORTER
                You'll be impressed reading my
                article how you brought equality
                to your railroad. How many women
                engineers do you have?

Executives at a loss for words. Female reporter points to
window. Executives spin around, see wives wave to them.
Executives swallow Adam's apples, bolt out the door SCREAMING.

                         PRESIDENT
                My train! They are stealing my
                brand new train!

Executives run to train as the SD-80's wind-up power. They
give up. IRON FACE arrives with a stretch-limo rigged with
auxiliary flange wheels. Executives scramble inside.

                         PRESIDENT
                      (continuing)
                Catch that train! That's my two-
                hundred-fifty-million-dollar
                train. Hurry-up!

SD-80's pour on the power, pull ahead rapidly. Limo races on
track, gaining.

INT. PRIVATE CAR / AUBURN - DAY

YVONNE speaks to three WOMEN sitting on lavish couches. A
royal interior decoration scheme.

                         YVONNE
                A chance of a lifetime. Well, are
                you in or out?

                         FIRST WOMAN
                Sounds good to me. Why not?

                         SECOND WOMAN
                This is preposterous, though
                highly stimulating.

                         THIRD WOMAN
                I'd love to!

Yvonne opens closet, flings filthy men's clothes. They
undress.

BACK TO SCENE

Limo gains on private car. LADIES stand by back door, open
pocketbooks, throw items on track, lipstick, mirror, perfume.
YVONNE pours mineral oil.

                         IRON FACE
               Look! Bums! Dirty bums!

Executives look hard.

                         THIRD EXECUTIVE
               That's my wife, Martha! She
               finally made good on her threats
               to run off with bums. Hey, that's
               your wife too, Mr. President.

Iron Face slams brakes, wheels slide on slick mineral oil.
Private car passes though crossing as flashing signal arms
descend DING! DING! Freight train approaches, air horns
HONK! THUNDERING engines RUMBLE through the crossing.

                         PRESIDENT
               Stop this blasted thing! Look
               out! Oh, no!

Men SCREAM. Arms cover faces KA-BOOM! Limo ruptures
CRYOGENIC FLUIDS tankcar. Escaping liquid flashes to white
gas cloud, blows limo backwards then jerks to a stop, frozen
in ice.

Tankcar rolls along track, sprays trees with white snow.
Raven flies from a tree into the snowy mist and exits frozen,
white wings extended, glides over limo.

INT. LIMO - DAY

Windows frosted. MEN shiver, exhale cold vapors. President
grabs door handle, it SNAPS off. Kicks the door, foot
punches through. Pushes door, CREAKS open. Foot still in
door, he awkwardly steps out of vehicle. Withdraws foot from
door.

                         PRESIDENT
               Darn it, darn it, darn it!

He kicks limo, it shatters like glass. Three men sit in a
pile of steaming rubble. Iron Face in a boiling rage.

                         SECOND EXECUTIVE
                    (to President)
               I told you it's bad luck to bring
               wives on the line.

Freight train clears tracks, crossing arms rise DING! DING!
DING!

INT. BALDWIN CAB / EAST APPLEGATE - DAY

DICK kicks firedoor closed. CLIFF opens firedoor. DONNY
sweats like a madman, shovels coal into firebox. BILL and
NORMAN in engineer and fireman's seat frantically operate
valves and levers.

                    BILL
          More steam! I need more steam!

                    DICK
          Faster, Donny. Faster, you can do
          it.

                    DONNY
          Bloody slavedriver. I'm doing the
          best I can.

                    NORMAN
          Steam. I want more steam! Give...
          me... steam!

Pressure gage rises to 175 psi, kisses red zone. They enter
mountains, pine trees flip past cab. Dick smiles ear-to-ear,
face in the wind.

EXT. NEW ENGLAND MILLS / SIERRA'S - NIGHT

BUMS sit on blankets by a campfire. Chit-chat talk reminds us
of people in a restaurant. TRIO, HARRY, FRANK, BILL and
NORMAN sit together near Baldwin engine.

                    HARRY
          Cliff, give me back, Marie. I
          need her.

Cliff hugs the tiny bottle. They Tub-O-War. Harry slaps
Cliff's hands, he wins. Harry slips chain over his head,
places vial down shirt. Cliff sulks.

                    HARRY
                 (continuing)
          Before the sun rises, you shall
          have your own flea.

Cliff smiles with expectation.

Bearded MASTER BUM appears from the forest dressed in a red
robe, silver wreathe in hair, gold staff in hand. Two BUMS
with lit red fusee's escort - One in a white tunic, other in
pink.

Crowd hushes. Bums stunned, like children seeing Santa.
Master stands by fire, scans crowd, locks eyes with a BUM.
Bum backs away as if a force of energy repulsed him.

Master spreads palms to sky as a praying monk. BUM applauds.
Bums restrain his hands.

                    MASTER
          We gather here tonight not as men,
          but as disturbed children in
          search of mothers to fulfill our
          inner desires.

CLIFF frowns, looks to FRANK.

                    CLIFF
          What's he talking about?

                    MASTER
               (angry, to Cliff)
          Thou dare to speak?

Bums rudely eyeball Cliff. Cliff cowers, shakes head.
Frank rises, apologizes, respectfully bows, then sits. DICK
and DONNY nervous. Dick looks for Mc'Corkle.

                    DICK
               (to Donny)
          We're one bum short. Mc'Corkle.

                    DONNY
          Ain't seen him. Don't care to.

                    MASTER
               (continuing speech)
          A woo-man dissolves men's souls
          who lust for the flesh. Your
          inner consciousness screams for
          relief from your inexperience, and
          raw amateur foolishness.

Fire POPS a gold sparkling amber skyward, lands in a BUM's
hair. He doesn't realize it.

                    MASTER
               (continuing)
          He who is guiltless, make yourself
          known so we may punish you.

Bum with burning amber in hair leaps up, SCREAMS, holds his
head in pain, dashes into forest.

                    BUM
          Yaaagh! Stop! Stop! Your
          searing my conscious mind!

Showers of smoke and sparks fizzle from his hair. Bums
MURMUR.

                    BILL
          Master, we have money, success,
          material wealth which dreams are
          made of. Please teach us to be at
          one with happiness.

Crowd murmurs in agreement.

                    MASTER
          My children, you have mindless
          constipation, piles of worry,
          impotence of heart and prostrated
          dreams of misery. PMS. Post
          marital psychosis. I tell you all,
          a woo-man cannot fathom the
          intimate needs of a man! They
          don't understand mankind's inner
          emotional feelings and desires.

Crowd nods approvingly.

                    DONNY
               (whispers to Dick)
          He's full of wisdom.

A BUM adjusts donut cushion he sits on, winces in pain.
Dick's eyes locked on Master with hopeful expression.

                    NORMAN
          Your Highness, we know this. Show
          us a sign so we may learn the way.

Master turns quickly, eyes reflect orange flames. Whips right
hand skyward, fingers shake. Bearded BUM dressed in pink
tunic hands him a beer. He swallows nonstop, tosses bottle
over shoulder. Flipping bottle fades into the darkness.
CLUNK!

                    A MAN'S VOICE (V.O.)
          Ow!

                    DICK
          Master, I hunger.

Master approaches, compassion in eyes, affectionately lays
hand on Dick's head, mumbles with quivering lips, sounds
like, "My son the beer is warm."

Dick looks up appearing as a remorseful child. Master
returns, stands by the fire.

Master twiddles fingers. Bum in white tunic hands him a
basket. Master gives the basket to CLIFF. Cliff removes a
pretzel, bites it with reverence, then passes basket on to
next bum. Cliff, barefooted, leaps up.

                    CLIFF
          It's a miracle! A miracle!

                    MASTER
          Sit down, fool!

Cliff sits, he explains to others,

                    CLIFF
          I just know I can deal with my
          wife now, I feel it in my balls.

He rubs the balls of his bare feet.

                    MASTER
          What am I to do with you? Why are
          you here? No, I tell you all.
          Woo-men enslave us. Tell us what
          to do. Keep us in debt and we
          need that!

Donny jams elbow into Cliff's rib OUCH!

                    DONNY
          What's that imbecile saying we
          need comforting molestation?

                    MASTER
               (to Donny)
          Silence, infidel! You shall not
          speak less spoken to. This is the
          law.

Dick stands, waves hand. Master permits him to speak.

                    DICK
          Master, you proclaim good things
          and speak of laws. I came to
          escape rules and regulations. I
          have a wife who is fiercely
          demanding and now I feel boxed in.
          Where can I find freedom if I
          can't find it here?

                    MASTER
          Behold this man speaks truth. You
          are all here because you heard the
          call of the wild, to be free of
          the chains of life, to walk in the
          footpath of those before us who
          dared to ride the iron spiked road
          to happiness and bliss.

Dick sits. Donny, Dick, Cliff hug each other. MC'CORKLE
rises from far edge of crowd. Dick's expression is one of
suspicion.

                    MC'CORKLE
                 (to the Master)
            Excuse me, I need to fix a leak.

He steps into the woods. Angry WOMAN'S faces peek from
trees, stare sternly at the congregation of bums.

                    MASTER
            I know the pain and heartache you
            kind and gentle men feel when you
            are home, seeing your wife
            fumbling the pages of sex
            magazines gawking in sinful
            centerfolds of scantily-clad men,
            while you sulk in the kitchen
            preparing diner. Tears dripping
            into the spaghetti sauce.

Bums wipe tears from eyes, blow noses. Trio's WIVES faces
loom in the woods, ablaze in fervent anger.

                    CLIFF
            Master, my wife doesn't understand
            my pain, failure, grief and guilt.
            She stopped loving me. She
            refuses to cuddle or talk to me
            after having sex. All I want in
            my marriage is equality. To be
            appreciated.

                    MASTER
            You ask much, my son. For
            centuries man has sought answers
            to the high-heeled pit-bulls we
            marry. My devastated, long-
            suffering child. Listen to me.
            You are doing the right thing. I
            feel your anger, pain and
            rejection. It is better to dwell
            in the wilderness than with a
            contentious bitch.

Master lays hand on ROGER'S head. More angry WOMEN's faces
appear among the dark forest.

                    MASTER
                 (continuing)
            He's a sick boy. A bitter case of
            the nuptials. It's a slow death,
            agony, pure unadulterated
            suffering. Don't do it my son.

              TOM
      Master, how did you know we yearn
      for women?

              MASTER
      You have no gray hair.

BUM with hair in flames SCREAMS, charges out of woods.

              DONNY
      Master, just once, just once, I'd
      like to hear my wife when she
      comes home tell me, "Darling
      that's beautiful. You dusted the
      windows and mopped the floor."

Donny wipes tears. Others pat him on shoulder.

              BUMS
        (randomly)
      "She doesn't know it hurts me." "I
      hate it when my wife does that."
      "I should be enough to satisfy
      her!"

              MASTER
      What is missing? A sense of
      purpose. A bonafide reason to
      live. We have plenty to live on,
      but nothing to live for.

            FEMALE VOICE
        (from woods)
      You lying sonofabitch!

Master spins around. Bums scared. Trio rise. Sound of
chains RATTLE, WOMEN surge from woods. Woman in high-heels
tackles Master with a flying leap, knocks him down. She grabs
his beard, drags him over campfire OUCH! His robe catches
fire.

            BUMS IN CROWD
      Wives! Wives! Run for your lives!

Women grab husbands, slap, pinch, kick them in butt. One
picks up a SCREAMING bum, twirls him over her head. Fat
WOMAN sits on husband, spanks him, hard.

                         WOMEN
                    (randomly)
          "I'm sick of this bum business and
          your escapades leaving me with the
          kids." "Get your miserable ass
          home and back to work." "I'll
          show you just how much I
          understand your innermost
          desires." "Does this hurt your
          feelings sweetheart?"

YVONNE, CHRISTINE, DEBBIE bolt on scene, see Trio slip into
the woods at a full run with the remaining bums.

Captured bums hooked to chains, dragged by their wives like
a prison chain gang. They beg for understanding and mercy.

FRANK and HARRY watch from a distance. They look sad.

                         HARRY
          Nobody wants us.

                         FRANK
          I know.

They pick up hobo sticks, walk into the dark forest.

Looking into the fire. PULL BACK - Old shoes. WIDER -
MC'CORKLE stands, warms hands by the fire. YVONNE,
CHRISTINE, DEBBIE approach him.

                         YVONNE
          We paid you to bring'em in. We
          made a deal. You didn't deliver.

                         MC'CORKLE
          I have them on the run. The man
          who fears suffering is already
          suffering from what he fears.

                         DEBBIE
          That's not good enough. They must
          be physically punished.

                         MC'CORKLE
          Don't tell me how to run my
          business.

                         CHRISTINE
                    (in his face)
          I'll show you how women run our
          business.

INT. FOREST - NIGHT

TRIO, HARRY, and FRANK rest. BUMS in chains straggle behind
rolling engines with headlights on. NORMAN and BILL captured
by WIVES.

                    DICK
               (to Frank)
          Why don't they leave us alone? Why
          won't they just let us live happy?
          I never thought Yvonne would chase
          me like this.

                    FRANK
          A woman's scorn ignites the fires
          of hell. She will not rest until
          she is vindicated.

Cliff's ears strain, eyes nervously search the woods.

                    DICK
          This is getting wretched. Marriage
          isn't supposed to be like this.
          A man needs room to breathe.
          What's wrong with that? Tell me.
          What the Dicken's do we do now?

Dick glances, frowns.

                    HARRY
          You run for your lives. That's
          what a good bum would do, and must
          do. If he wants to remain a
          living bum.

                    FRANK
          Freedom has a price. You don't
          want to pay do you? You think
          running away can solve all of your
          problems, well it doesn't. It
          only creates more, and often more
          than you bargained for.

Dick flinches.

                    DONNY
               (to Dick)
          Hey, I thought this was the life
          of Tom Sawyer?

                              FRANK
                    Mark Twain wrote the chapter,
                    revealing the secret of escape,
                    but legend claims his wife stole
                    it from the manuscript. It never
                    got published. Bums have been
                    striving to discover the secret
                    ever since. That's what it's all
                    about. We are all still searching.

                              DICK
                    What is this? Some kind of
                    experiment gone bad? I don't know
                    and I don't care about books and
                    secret plans. I'm here to fulfill
                    my childhood dreams and nobody is
                    going to stop me.

Donny and Cliff nod with approval.

INT. AMTAK / PASSENGER CAR / CAPE HORN TUNNEL- DAY

GRANDMOTHER (85) knits sweater. Adjacent seat, three OLD MEN
(80's) read newspapers. Train enters tunnel, lights out.

MOMENTS LATER

Train exits tunnel, lights on. Grandmother happily knits,
HUMS a tune. Three exhausted old men button shirts and
belts. Newspapers scattered over floor. Lipstick on faces.

EXT. MOUNTAINS / YUBA RIVER - DAY

BUMS skinny-dip. BUM on a bluff blows sheep's HORN.

Bums scatter. Diesel smoke puffs above a ridge. Engine THROBS
echo on canyon walls. AMTAK engines clawing its way up the
pass.

BACK TO SCENE / INSIDE AMTAK PASSENGER CAR - DAY

WOMEN excited, point to windows, see BEARS on hind legs, herd
of DEER drinking water by Yuba river. Women take pictures.

                              WOMAN
                    Oh, look. Wildlife.

Amtak snakes around a curve out of view.

EXT. YUBA RIVER - DAY

Bears and deer hiss PSSSST! Wrinkle and fold as they
deflate. TRIO, FRANK, HARRY's heads poke out. Harry holds
deer's head under arm, approaches Dick in a bear suit.

                              HARRY
                    Works every time.

EXT. COLFAX / SIERRA FOOTHILLS - DAY

SD-80's pull in to depot. WIVES step out, disguised in bum
clothing. Baldwin on siding. BUM leans against depot,
watches closely as they walk. LADIES in private car step
into engine cab, drive train out.

YVONNE, CHRISTINE, DEBBIE approach the Bum.

          YVONNE
           (gruff voice)
    Excuse me brother, where's the
    action?

          BUM
    This is Colfax. Ain't no action
    here 'cept trains comin'go. They
    come and go, go and come. Can
    drive ya loony.

Wives walk a dirt trail into forest. Scenery changes.
Yellow grass along trail turns green. Pine trees replaced by
Italian Cypress, lush flowers. Trail changes to stones.

          DEBBIE
    We must be entering somebody's
    arboretum. We won't find them
    here. Lets turn back.

See a signpost, "The Appian Way."

          YVONNE
    I've never seen this in travel
    magazines.

          CHRISTINE
    I can sense his presence. He's
    here, I just know Donny is here.

          DEBBIE
    How do you know? Woman's
    intuition?

          CHRISTINE
    No, it's vibrating. It does that
    when Donny is near.

Yvonne and Debbie recoil with embarrassment.

          YVONNE
    This is no time for romantic
    fantasies.

          CHRISTINE
    Fantasies my ass!

Christine pulls out a directional finder. Needle points to a small rise a few feet away.

                    YVONNE
          You little stinker. Where did you
          get that thing?

                    CHRISTINE
          Elise gave it to me. Here I come,
          honeybuns.

They approach the rise, look down, stunned, see ancient Rome. Marble buildings graced with black iron and gold statues.

Chariots rumble in streets past magnificent fountains. The celebrated monument to Victor Emmanuel II near the coliseum.

                    YVONNE
          Sooo, this is why they left us.

HONK! HONK! Wives turn. White goose, fig leaves on head, neck low to ground, charges them. They SCREAM, dash over the rise to,

INT. ROME - DAY

WIVES run into city. Angry gander sees female with a pink ribbon around neck. He stops, nuzzles her.

Wives, breathless, step through Arch of Constantine, enter the gardens, stroll by Rometta Square fountains, Draghi fountain, Ovato fountain. Then into the Forum.

Wide-eyed wives see men in head wreathes, white togas, greeting each other. All in a state of bliss. Men lounge in hot springs, others dine under Egyptian palms. CENTURIONS guard steps of buildings.

                    YVONNE
          I don't see any women. This has
          got to be a bum encampment. Keep
          a sharp eye. They're here.

MAN hails a taxi. Chariot arrives. Man leaves.

EXT. ROW OF STATUES - DAY

Six MIDGETS, painted white, put on solid rock shoes resembling feet. They argue with a CENTURION.

                    MIDGET
          I don't want to work overtime. My
          feet ache. Plus I have a train to
          catch to Reno tonight.

Centurion places hand on Midget's shoulder.

                          CENTURION
                 We're short of staff. I promise
                 you, Art. I'll have you guys
                 relief in one hour, okay? Do it
                 for Caesar.

ART approaches a statue. It comes to life, steps down.

                          STATUE
                 See you next shift, stiff.

Midgets grumble under their breath, step onto marble
pedestals. They hold their pose. One is a gold CUPID.
Another statue pees in a clamshell basin.

BACK TO SCENE

WIVES stroll by a row of headless naked female statues.
SCULPTOR in b.g. chisels a new female statue's head.

                          YVONNE
                 Even here they show contempt for
                 women. Disguise your voices.

Sculptor in b.g. with hammer whacks head off the statue. He
pinches his fingers together, kisses them, "Beautiful."

                          CHRISTINE
                 So, that's why statues in Rome are
                 missing heads!

They stop by Midget statues.

                          DEBBIE
                 Cute buns on this one.

DEBBIE reaches to statue's rear. YVONNE grabs her hand, nods
to sign, "Don't Touch Art." Debbie by a peeing statue.
Places hand in yellow water.

                          DEBBIE
                       (continuing)
                 Golly, that's warm water.

She cups hands, sips water. Her eyes light up.

                          DEBBIE
                       (continuing)
                 Tastes like wine.

Inscription on pedestal, "God Of The Grapes." She feels
statue's foot, raps knuckles on it.

                          DEBBIE
                       (continuing)
                 Ow! Solid marble.

Midget statue smiles.

EXT. ORGAN'S FOUNTAIN - DAY

TRIO, FRANK, HARRY bathing in fountain. Snapping turtle
clamps on Donny's toe OUCH!

                         DICK
                    (panic)
               Turtles!

ROMAN'S laugh as they run and dive into the fountain of
Trevi. Sign, "Turtle Out To Lunch."

BACK TO SCENE

WIVES by a circular somber stone, hollow eyes and mouth - The
Mouth of Truth. Chiseled inscription, "Tell Me The Truth."
Christine touches its face, pokes finger in right eye.

                         DEBBIE
               Talk to it. Legend claims it bites
               the hand that lies to it.

                         CHRISTINE
               I don't believe that hogwash.

                         YVONNE
               Go ahead, put your fingers in its
               mouth and lie to it.

                         CHRISTINE
               I don't believe this. You do it.

                         YVONNE
               I believe. You're the one who
               doubts it. Oh, so you're scared
               of a fable?

Debbie and Yvonne LAUGH. Christine inserts fingers.

                         CHRISTINE
               When I catch, Donny. I'm going to
               give him a big juicy kiss.

Stone's mouth closes, clamps hard OUCH!

                         CHRISTINE
                    (continuing)
               Get it off me. Get it off me.

ROMANS pass by, shake heads in disgust.

                         DEBBIE
                    (to stone,
                     apologizing)
               She deserves it. It's okay.

Stone lets go. Christine hops around. Stone smiles. Bee
buzzes and stings CUPID, accidentally releases arrow BOING!

EXT. COLISEUM / ARENA - DAY

Two GLADIATORS, TOM with net and trident, ROGER with spiked
iron ball and shield whacking it out. Crowd CHEERS. Roger
jumps as net swings under feet, sidesteps trident jabs.

EXT. COLISEUM PODIUM - DAY

CAESAR sits, shakes head, disgusted, it's CASEY, thumb points
down. SKINNER in a Queen's gown, files fingernails, veil on
face, pouting.

                    SKINNER
          Next year I'm going to be Caesar.

                    CASEY
          Silence, bitch!

Skinner's lips purse, resumes filing fingernails.

BACK TO SCENE

                    ROGER
          I told you we should have gone to
          Caesar's palace. Now look at the
          mess you got us into.

Roger swings iron ball, Tom ducks.

                    TOM
          I thought this was Caesar's palace.

Tom swings net, misses, trident tears Roger's sandals OUCH!
CROWD in an uproar, stand up SCREAMING.

DARLENE and KAREN disguised as Senators, CHEER with the
crowd. MC'CORKLE nearby, hollers with thumb down.

                    DARLENE
          Golly, those two bums look like a
          million bucks.

                    KAREN
          I like the one with the iron ball
          and net. He's the one who will
          marry me. Only he doesn't know it
          yet.

Cupid's arrow flies into arena sticks in Roger's butt OUCH!
Darlene and Karen stand terrified as Roger pounds iron ball
on Tom's trident, stumbles, falls, ball crashes inches from
Tom's head into dirt. Crowd LAUGHS, lions released, chase
Tom and Roger into,

INT. GLADIATOR CHANGING ROOM - DAY

GLADIATORS inside. ROGER and TOM wash up.

             ROGER
    You were trying to kill me.

             TOM
    That's show business, Roger.
    Anyway, I seen them. They were
    sitting with the Republicans.

             ROGER
    You ruined my sandals.

Roger's sandals look like coiled springs. They put on black
leather shorts, black suspenders crisscross back and chests.
Huge gold belt buckle engraved with gladiators fighting.

They look in mirror, adjust gold wreathes on heads. SLAVE
approaches, hands them a note. GLADIATOR approaches.

             GLADIATOR
    If that's what I think it is, you
    guys are in for trouble.

INT. DEMETRIUS GIFT SHOP - DAY

WIVES enter. DEMETRIUS behind counter.

             DEMETRIUS
    I don't have anymore gold
    wreathes. Plum sold out. May I
    suggest figleaf swim wear? Won't
    wilt, shrivel or dissolve for two
    days. Guaranteed.

He dangles a G-string with a green leaf. CHRISTINE peruses
dolls, picks up Caesar, pulls a string.

             CAESAR DOLL
    My name is Caesar. And I run
    whenever I see her.

DEBBIE lifts rolls of brown toilet paper tied to a leather
thong. YVONNE fingers a sword blade.

             DEBBIE
    How much are these papyrus tissues?

             DEMETRIUS
    Ah! I see you have fine taste.
    Cleopatra brand is the finest
    silver can buy. One denarius.

                          DEBBIE
                That's twenty-five denarii.

                          YVONNE
                We'll shop around.

                          DEMETRIUS
                Sooner or later I'll be seeing
                you. The only shop in Rome.

Yvonne and Debbie approach Christine. She's twists the head
off Caesar. Pulls string again.

                          CAESAR DOLL
                My name is Caesar and Cleopatra
                never tells me to take out the
                trash.

Three CENTURIONS enter, block exit, withdraw swords. Wives
petrified, back up against doll rack, porcelain bust of
Caesar tumbles, crumbles on Christine's head. Centurions
advance.

                          CENTURION
                     (to Demetrius)
                Can you sharpen our swords today?

Wives hightail out. Yvonne grabs three figleaf G-strings.

                          DEMETRIUS
                     (to wives)
                Hey, you busted my bust.

Centurions pursue. Wives run down cobblestone street, duck
into graveyard. Centurions run by. Wives enter a cave.

INT. CATACOMBS - DAY

                          DEBBIE
                Look. These are real graves.

They walk along wiping cobwebs from catacombs, read the
names. Names of Mrs. only. No men.

                          DEBBIE
                     (continuing)
                Look at this. New ones.

DEBBIE waves as YVONNE and CHRISTINE approach three new white
marble vaults. They SCREAM seeing their name and year of
birth. They explode with hostility seeing, "Year of
death" - "Soon."

EXT. COBBLESTONE STREET - DAY

Three CENTURIONS hear SCREAMS from storm drain.

                           CENTURION
                    Catacombs!

Centurions run, trip on swords, fall down.

BACK TO SCENE

WIVES pound fists on covers, SCREAM. CENTURIONS run at them.
Wives dash deep into the darkness, split up in tunnels.
Centurions split up.

CHRISTINE makes a ghostly WOOING sound. Centurion backs away.
DEBBIE places her hand on Christine's and YVONNE'S shoulder
YIKES! They run in separate directions. Centurions plow
head-on, fall to ground.

MOMENTS LATER

YVONNE in centurion uniform ties up the three naked
Centurions, each wears a fig leaf. DEBBIE and CHRISTINE slip
into Centurion uniforms.

EXT. STREET - DAY

TRIO bathe under waterfall, see three CENTURIONS approach,
swords drawn. They duck under water. Three hands search for
them, one is black, pulls their hair.

Three MALE CENTURIONS drag them out, scold them. Down the
street, WIVES approach, see husbands.

                           YVONNE
                    Seize those bums!

TRIO run away, wear figleafs and wreathes. They hop into
chariot taxi, race down the street. Wives hail a taxi.
Horse stomps Christine's foot OUCH! They hop in.

                           YVONNE
                         (continuing)
                    Follow that taxi.

Chariots race through forum, Roman CITIZENS part a path, Dick
swipes a string of pomegranates from market. Post on market
yanked away, awning collapses on SHOPPERS.

                           DICK
                    Faster. Faster! They are gaining.

                           DRIVER
                    Who's they?

DRIVER glances over shoulder, "Yikes"

                         DRIVER
                    (continuing; to Dick)
                You broke your vows. Women can't
                come here.

EXT. THE APPIAN WAY - DAY

Road lined with Italian Cypress. Trio crash through matte
glass scenery painting. Scenery now of ancient Egypt,
pyramids, palm shrouded Nile river.

Road gives way, chariot falls, rips through canvas painted
ground.

EXT. WIVES CHARIOT - DAY

DRIVER pulls emergency brake. Horses feet gallop in reverse.
Places sandal on iron rim of wheel, burns foot OUCH! He
jumps out, lands in sand dune. Horses swing in a circle.
Chariot dangles on edge of cliff. WIVES SCREAM.

EXT. TRIO'S CHARIOT - DAY

TRIO tumble into safety net. Net fails, fall into a pile of
brown mud. Cart heaped with mud exits barn, approaches.

Lettering on cart, "Diocletian's Barn Cleaning Services."
Cart lifts like a dumptruck, pours manure on them.

EXT. LONG RAVINE / UNDER BRIDGE - AFTERNOON

TRIO, FRANK, HARRY bathe under waterfall. Ten-engine freight
train passes over bridge, takes "S" turns at full throttle.

                         DICK
                Where's your wives?

                         FRANK
                Bachelor. Wife left years ago.

                         DICK
                I'm sorry. I mean, you're lucky.

                         HARRY
                Never wanted another woman.
                They're always complaining about
                something. But sometimes I feel --

                         DONNY
                Christine's never happy. She's a
                slavemaster. Why are they always
                bitchin' all the time?

                         FRANK
                Nature of the beast.

                         CLIFF
          Debbie delights and relishes
          telling me what to do. I mean she
          really enjoys being a CEO. Irks
          me to no end. I hate it. Who put
          them in charge anyway?

                         DICK
          I'm not going back, ever. This is
          my world, my life, my dream. The
          wives are intruding and it's time
          we get them out of here. No
          matter what it takes. I'm tired
          of running. When I see her she's
          going to have to deal with the new
          Dick Crossmaheart!

Two PILGRIMS with matchlock rifles step from woods, wicks
smoke on rifles, point guns at them.

                    FIRST PILGRIM
          What bringeth ye to thee falls?

Trio huddles tightly.

                         FRANK
          Brother. We seek ye refuge.

                    SECOND PILGRIM
          Come with I.

They stand, step on a rock engraved, "Plymouth Rock West."
They leave with the Pilgrims.

EXT. PLYMOUTH VILLAGE / GOLD RUN - DAY

PILGRIMS busily fix straw-thatched roofs, sell goods, typical
community. INDIANS carry bottles of cranberry juice on
poles. TRIO, FRANK, HARRY greet pilgrims, stroll to,

EXT. INT. PLYMOUTH VILLAGE / THATCH HUT - DAY

TRIO, FRANK, HARRY enter thatch hut. PILGRIM opens closet,
removes Pilgrim clothes.

                    FIRST PILGRIM
          Yea, this is good?

TRIO exit in Pilgrim clothes. Donny polishes his buckled
shoes with knuckle.

                         DONNY
          Christine will never recognize me
          in this disguise.

They walk through the village, come upon a PILGRIM plucking
white feathers from a SQUAWKING turkey. DONNY stops, others
walk on.

                         DONNY
                    (continuing)
              Why do thee pluck ye wretched
              beast?

                         PILGRIM
              Discipline thee. Clucky dranketh
              me potion.

                         DONNY
              Clucky?

                         PILGRIM
              Me pet.
                    (to turkey)
              Yee bad bird.
                    (to Donny)
              Drink of thy cup?

Pilgrim releases half-bald turkey, reaches for a wood bowl,
gives it to Donny. He sniffs the moldy red fluid, nose
shrivels as if it were ammonia.

                         PILGRIM
                    (continuing)
              Drink ye. Good for ye.

Donny closes eyes, gulps contents, face contorts. He spins
around, faces Pilgrim. Pilgrim holds up white painted
mirror. Donny's face aghast with horror seeing his face pure
white.
                         PILGRIM
                    (continuing)
              Do not worry thee. Lasts only a
              dawn. Sufficient time for thee to
              flee.

Donny skips off to join the others. They look at him as if
nothing has happened. Pilgrim wipes talcum powder off mirror.

                         DONNY
              Look at me. Look. I've changed.
              Christine will never recognize me
              now.

                         DICK
              Donny, grow up.

Pilgrim stops at edge of forest, waves. Trio, Frank and
Harry hike into forest, follow yellow brick road.

EXT. YELLOW BRICK ROAD - DUSK

TRIO, FRANK and HARRY pass spooky apple trees, hollow faces.
Owl HOOTS, swoops low, rips hair from Donny's head OUCH!
Frank raises arm. They stop. Frank crawls up a small rise,
looks over edge, waves.

WHAT THEY SEE - OLD BUMS (70's) by boxcars strung with
flashing neon lights, "Girls! Girls! Girls!", "Arcade",
"Casino", "Hospital". Trees glitter with Christmas lights.

                    DICK
          Fantastic! Let's go.

They walk along boxcars flabbergasted by the electrical
parade of lights. Peek into the "Girls" car, loud rock
music, topless STRIPPERS (40's) dance, drunken BUMS clap,
howl.

BOUNCER (90) approaches holding a sparking taser gun.

                    BOUNCER
          Tickets?

Harry pulls out a string of tickets, tears off five.

INT. GIRLS BOXCAR - NIGHT

BUMS dressed in outfits to fit their fantasy. A General,
Knight, Bum in diaper, Cop, Centurion, Scottish skirts, etc.

                    DICK
          Female impersonator show?

                    FRANK
          Real thing.

                    DICK
          Thought you guys had a code of
          decency?

                    HARRY
          For entertainment only. This is
          where old strippers retire. We
          fulfill their dreams. Make them
          feel young again. What's wrong
          with that?

EXT. ON THE MOUNTAIN RIDGE - NIGHT

WIVES gaze down at the colorful glittering boxcars.

                    YVONNE
          I'm gonna kill him!

                    CHRISTINE
          But first we got to catch'em.

                              DEBBIE
                    I have an idea.

INT. GIRLS BOXCAR - NIGHT

TRIO drinking, taunt the DANCERS, "Take it off." Show ends,
ladies stumble behind stage curtain.

YVONNE, CHRISTINE, DEBBIE appear on stage, dance to sexy
saxophone MUSIC. Trio's eyes widen.

                              DONNY
                    The, the, that's our wives!

DICK spits drink, sprays CLIFF. BUMS scream, "Take it off."
Dick makes his way to BARTENDER, whispers in ear. Bartender
steps behind stage, locks stage door. Dick slyly smiles at
Yvonne.

                              YVONNE
                    It's not work...ing.

                              DEBBIE
                    I thought they would stop us.

                              CHRISTINE
                    Now look at the mess you got us
                    into. What are we going to do?

DEBBIE dances backwards, tries doorknob. Bums BOO and HISS.
She dances back between Yvonne and Christine.

                              DEBBIE
                    The dirty bums locked the door!

Bums place their tiny bottles and chains on dance floor.
Wives step on them, fleas leap. They scratch and dance
wildly. Cliff steals one.

                              CHRISTINE
                    Nobody boo's me. I'll show them
                    what a woman really looks like!

Christine swirls her hips. Bums CHEER in a frenzy.

                              DEBBIE
                    We've got to get out of here.

                              YVONNE
                    Enjoy it. Nobody's going to know
                    back home.

Yvonne flings her blouse to the screaming bums. She smiles,
puckers her lips like a sex kitten.

                              YVONNE
                         (continuing)
                    I like this. They really
                    appreciate us.

Wives kick shoes into audience. Bums scramble for them.
Christine's shoe smacks Donny square on forehead, stuns him.

DICK walks from bar to Cliff and Donny.

                              DICK
                    I don't like reruns.

Trio step out, leave FRANK and HARRY inside. They enter,

INT. CASINO BOXCAR - NIGHT

BUMS play slot machines, silver dollars clank loudly. Crap
table is hot, players CHEER.

DONNY throws craps, DICK and CLIFF at 21-card table. DEALER
deals a ten to Dick. Cliff doesn't play. He fondles his
little bottle with flea inside. Dick frowns.

                              DICK
                    Don't let that beast out of the
                    bottle.

Cliff swipes bottle close to his chest, protecting it. Nose
close to bottle.

                              CLIFF
                    Hello, there little, Diane.

Dick tries to grab bottle. Cliff shoves it down his shirt.

                              CLIFF
                         (continuing)
                    How come we're not running, Dick?
                    I don't want to get caught. We
                    must leave here.

Dick's picks finger, peels skin from thumb.

                              DICK
                    Don't worry about it. The spouses
                    are enjoying themselves.

                              CLIFF
                    They are?

                              DICK
                    Yep, getting attention,
                    recognition, appreciation,
                    everything they always wanted.
                    We'll be safe, for awhile.

> CLIFF
> I don't like my wife doing that.

Dick stares into card, scratches card on table, gets an ace.
Dealer grins. Slides "Ocean Breeze Brand Suppositories" for
payoff. Dick puts them in pocket.

> DICK
> Twenty-one. Let's do it again.

Deals again, same hand. Cliff nervously looks over shoulder.
Dick isn't smiling, still picking thumb. He watches as Cliff
strolls to slot machines, then he leaves, with ace card.
Walks to,

EXT. / INT. HOSPITAL BOXCAR - NIGHT

Sign, "Psychiatrist In Girly Car. Come Back Tomorrow"

DICK steps inside, compassion in his eyes. BUMS hooked to
enema bottles painfully MOAN and GROAN. NURSE clasps enema
bottle, patient HOWLS.

> FEMALE NURSE
> Spit it out. Spit it out.
> Where's my husband? Casey Jones!

Squeezes bottle with all her might YEOW! Enema bag POPS!

Dick steps outside,

EXT. BY BOXCARS - NIGHT

DICK hears patient SCREAM o.s. as he walks away, head down,
hands in pockets, kicks aluminum can, it fades into the dark
forest. HARRY approaches.

> DICK
> I feel an emptiness inside, like
> grasping a shadow, a persistent
> ache.

> HARRY
> A man's worst difficulties begin
> when he is able to do as he
> pleases.
>   (beat)
> You miss her?

> DICK
> I didn't think I would.

                    HARRY
          She won't forgive you until she
          punishes you. That's how they
          are. If I were you, I'd keep
          running. A woman's wrath is as
          potent as a viper's venom.

Harry walks away. Dick flicks ace card into forest. Harry
returns with Dick's Tom Sawyer outfit.

EXT. KENTUCKY GOLD MINE - SUNRISE

THUMP! THUMP! THUMP! WIVES in disguise, wear beards, hide in
bush, see BUMS push ore cart, dump ore to thumping stamp
mill. They sneak to a window, see ore pounded into dust under
the stamps. BUMS separate gold on corrugated copper recovery
tray.

                    DEBBIE
          So this is how they finance their
          fantasies. They've gotta bloody
          gold mine!

Steam WHISTLE blows. Bums leave. Crouching low, wives enter,

INT. KENTUCKY GOLD MINE - DAY

Lights stretch deep into the dark mine shaft.

                    SCRATCHY VOICE (V.O.)
          Hi, sweetie. Looking for something?

WIVES jolted, look up, see red PARROT dangling in a cage.

                    PARROT
          Help! Help! Wives invasion. Red
          alert. Fire in the hole.

BUM MINER peeks out of stope, screams, "Wives!" Pulls lever,
iron doors slam, wives trapped. Christine grabs cage bars,
spreads bars, reaches in.

                    CHRISTINE
          I'll pluck your feathers you
          double-crossing little --

Parrot bites her finger OW! Alarm rings DINGALING!

                    PARROT
          Awk! Bye-bye, bitch!

Parrot's beak yanks a string in cage BOOM! Sidewall
explodes, opens hole in wall.

Opposite wall - Small door opens, skunks enter. Wives dash
into hole in wall. Water sprays, they slip on a chute, exit
side of mountain, fall into river below.

EXT. / INT. BARN - DAY

WIVES trudge along trail, see a barn, step inside, see a
traveling MEDICINE WAGON inside. Cows MOO.

                    YVONNE
          I have a sensational idea.

EXT. DUTCH FLAT / SIERRA'S - DAY

Medicine wagon with no drivers glide on rails, cows pull
wagon. Inscription, "Milk And Cookies." BUMS stop cows,
look inside, raid it.

                    BUM
          Where's the blasted cookies!

Bums milk cows, push wagon on, then enter the woods.

EXT. DOWN THE ROAD - DAY

BUM approaches, peeks inside, it's MC'CORKLE. WIVES exit
floorboards, grab and gag him, tie him up with nylon
stockings. YVONNE snaps reins, "Giddy-up." Cows MOO as they
pull cart.

                    YVONNE
          Where's our husbands? It's time
          to deliver, Mc'Corkle.

                    MC'CORKLE
          I can't. I'd rather stick needles
          in my eyes than break my vows.

CHRISTINE twiddles fingers. DEBBIE pulls barrette from hair,
hands to Christine. Mc'Corkle's eyes wide, folds arms. Pin
approaches his eye. Yvonne grabs Christine's arm.

MOMENTS LATER

MC'CORKLE's pants down, over Yvonne's knee. She holds a huge
hypodermic needle.

                    YVONNE
          You lie, you'll cry. Tell mommy
          everything.

Mc'Corkle won't answer. Pouts like a child.

                    YVONNE
                    (continuing)
          So, ya wanna play doctor, huh?

She pricks his butt with needle OUCH! Debbie approaches with
soapy water, brush, perfume.

                         DEBBIE
               Let's give him a bath, do his
               hair, soak him in perfume, then
               release him. The bums will meter
               justice.

Mc'Corkle's face in total fear. Distant engines THROB o.s.

                         MC'CORKLE
               Okay. Okay. I'll talk.

They step out by ten idling GP-60M engines. Wives release
cows, push wagon. It rolls down the track. They drag
Mc'Corkle away.

EXT. BUTTE CANYON / TRESTLE AND TUNNEL - DAY

TRIO on trestle by tunnel. DICK inserts fuse cord, DONNY
drops dynamite in holes along face of the tunnel. CLIFF
unknowingly unwinds detonator cord across rail. FRANK and
HARRY cover ears and skedaddle.

                         DICK
               This is the only way.

EXT. R.R. TRACK BY TUNNEL ENTRANCE - DAY

Milkwagon speeds into tunnel.

BACK TO SCENE

TRIO stands on trestle, near detonator.

Wagon rushes out of tunnel, cuts detonator cord. DONNY pushes
detonator handle, nothing happens.

They run, wagon chases them on trestle. No escape, they
latch onto wagon, climb aboard.

INT. / EXT. MILKWAGON - DAY

DICK and CLIFF sit in drivers seat, terrified. DONNY in back,
curled into fetal position, sucks thumb. FRANK and HARRY
try, but can't catch the wagon.

EXT. TUNNEL ENTRANCE - DAY

Ten straining GP-60M's rounding curve, dives into tunnel.

BACK TO SCENE

Wagon accelerates, takes curves on two wheels, BUMS by tracks
wave as terrified TRIO pass by.

EXT. TUNNEL EXIT / ON TRESTLE - DAY

GP-60M's exit, MC'CORKLE tied to front of engine, arms and
legs stretched out, SCREAMING. WIVES in front windows, mean
and serious. Pass by BUMS, horrified what they see, they
scatter.

GP-60M's gains on wagon. DONNY peeks out back, frighten,
sees train, HORNS blaring, headlights bearing down.

                    DONNY
          Look out, spouse attack!

CLIFF and DICK toss milk containers on rail, bounce, whacks
engine, nearly hit Mc'Corkle, cracks engine windshield.
Smoke kicks from engines, gaining on wagon. Mc'Corkle sees
wagon closing, shuts his eyes, SCREAMS.

Engine bumps wagon, crushes back end, hits again, wheel
loose, wobbles. Dick leaps to engine, unties Mc'Corkle.
Cliff and Donny jump. Wagon falls apart, crushed under
engines wheels.

Men climb to top of engine, run along roof of engines and
boxcars. Signal bridge advances. They duck, just in time.

EXT. BUM ENCAMPMENT / FOREST - DAY

BUMS talk to FRANK and HARRY. Others snooze in brass beds.

                    FIRST BUM
          Frank, you got to help them.

                    FRANK
          You know the peril.

                    SECOND BUM
          We all know the risks, but we
          can't just stand by and do nothing.

                    HARRY
          Frank, we sponsored them. It's
          our responsibility.

                    FRANK
          They need to learn. If we bail
          them out they will never become
          true bums or earn their advanced
          degrees. Is that what you want?

EXT. GP-60M TRAIN - DAY

Engines enter tunnel, TRIO hug roofs. Choke, gasp on diesel
fumes. Exit tunnel, trio smeared with exhaust.

YVONNE, CHRISTINE exit cab, climb roof, grasps air hoses,
jump between engines, chase TRIO. DONNY'S foot punches
through roof, foot stuck. Ladies gain on them.

>   DONNY
>   Go. Save yourselves.

>   DICK
>   Your a hero, Donny.

>   CLIFF
>   I'll always remember you.

>   MC'CORKLE
>   Good-bye, dear brother.

They run, Christine whacks Donny's rear with hose. Yvonne
continues to chase Dick, Cliff, Mc'Corkle.

>   CHRISTINE
>   (to Donny)
>   Now, my love. Payback's a bitch.

>   DONNY
>   Please don't hurt me, honey. They
>   made me do it. I never wanted to
>   leave you. I'm so happy to see
>   you again.

>   CHRISTINE
>   I love you too. Sweetie!

She sits on his back, twiddles fingernails by his temples.

>   CHRISTINE
>   (continuing)
>   For better or for worse. You
>   remember that, Donald? Do you?

Pokes fingernails into Donny's skull, squeezes with all her
might, nails snap, Donny SCREAMS.

EXT. GP-60M BOXCAR ROOF - DAY

YVONNE gains on DICK and CLIFF now standing on caboose. Just
when she gets close, Dick pulls lever, uncouples caboose.
She throws hose at him, he ducks, misses, slams MC'CORKLE in
face. He falls down. Dick laughs.

INT. PALACE / ROME - DAY

KAREN, DARLENE, ROGER and TOM on balcony by gardens.

                    KAREN
          I'm not materialistic. I prefer
          the simple home life. I like to
          cook, sew, take care of my man.

Roger focusing on her boobs.

                    ROGER
          That's exactly what I look for in
          a woman.

                    KAREN
          My idea of a happy life is to
          serve my man everything his little
          heart desires. Expensive
          vacations, clothes, mansions don't
          turn me on.

Karen puckers her lips.

                    TOM
          What's a nice girl like you doing
          in a place like this?

                    DARLENE
          I thought I would meet a rich man,
          but now I know that's not for me.
          I want someone who will love me.
          A rich man loves his money. I'm
          leaving tomorrow. I'd rather live
          my life an old spinster than marry
          a man for money.

                    TOM
          But you are sooo, beautiful.

                    DARLENE
          Take me!

EXT. GP-60M TRAIN / CABOOSE ROOF - DAY

CLIFF cranks hand brake, squeals to a stop. MC'CORKLE throws
switch, DICK pushes caboose, rolls to,

EXT. BUM ENCAMPMENT / FOREST - DAY

FRANK and HARRY approach DICK, CLIFF, MC'CORKLE. BUMS SNORE
in brass beds under pine trees, hugging stuffed animals.

                    FRANK
          Where's Donny?

                    CLIFF
          Wives got him. We barely escaped
          ourselves.

                         HARRY
                    Frank, he's gonna talk.

                         FRANK
                         (to Dick)
                    It's your play, Dick. We can't
                    help you. You need to earn your
                    title or return to slavery. Only
                    you can make that decision. We
                    will respect it either way.

Dick picks his thumb, thinks hard.

                         DICK
                    Give ourselves up to save our
                    friend?

                         HARRY
                    The choice is yours. Donny will
                    understand even though he'll be in
                    hell the rest of his life.

Dick picks both thumbs, bites lower lip.

                         DICK
                    Donny accepted danger. We all
                    knew this could happen. It is
                    better for one to suffer for the
                    good of the many.

                         FRANK
                    Unless you are the one.

                         CLIFF
                    I ain't going back, Dick. I mean
                    it. I got bummin' in my blood.

                         MC'CORKLE
                    Freedom is ours. Take it and run
                    with it.

Dick's in deep thought. Sucks thumb.

                         HARRY
                         (to Dick)
                    Ya got the makin's to be a good
                    bum.

EXT. BUM ENCAMPMENT / DONNER PASS / HIGH SIERRA - DAY

Light snowfall. BUMS heat coffee on track switch. Rub hands
over switch rails warming them.

IRON FACE in white jeep, yellow light flashes on roof, comes
around curve, sees bums, accelerates. Bums run. Iron Face
stops, steps out by switch.

>   IRON FACE
>   (yells at bums)
>   Thanks for the coffee, suckers.

Shivering bums look sad as Iron Face sips their coffee, kicks
the pot into the snow.

>   IRON FACE
>   (continuing)
>   Stay off my switch heaters.

Iron Face reaches for radio in jeep.

>   IRON FACE
>   (continuing)
>   Traffic control, Trainmaster one.
>   Switch mile marker six five, hot.

>   VOICE ON RADIO (V.O.)
>   Traffic control, train dispatcher
>   reports cold switch at six-seven
>   miles.

Jeep speeds up the road. Arrives at cold switch. Pots, pans,
trash littered on track switch, switch frozen with ice. Iron
Face removes shotgun and electrical fuses from jeep.

>   IRON FACE
>   Infernal bums! More trouble than
>   thar worth. There's the culprit.

Sees burnt coffee pot on switch. Kicks it. BLASTS ice from
switch with shotgun. Slips fuses in fusebox, throws switch,
ice melts. Stares meanly into woods.

EXT. SKI SLOPE - DAY

Snow falls. BUMS ride sleds, saucers, and toboggans, laugh
like kids. BOOM! BOOM! They hear shotgun blast echo o.s.
DICK shakes FRANK and HARRY'S hand.

>   DICK
>   We must leave now.

MC'CORKLE and CLIFF hug Frank, Harry. They walk into
snowstorm, wear snowshoes, carry hobo sticks over shoulders
and fade into the blizzard.

>   HARRY
>   Many are called, few are chosen.

>   FRANK
>   I had high hopes for them.

Frank and Harry drag toboggan up hill.

EXT. SNOWSHED / YUBA GAP - NIGHT

DICK, CLIFF, MC'CORKLE run out of snowshed just as ten SD-
40's exit, HORN blows. Engines pound hard. SWOOSH!

                    MC'CORKLE
          I know where Donny is.

                    DICK
          You do? How would you know? Are
          you some kind of detective?

                    MC'CORKLE
          Your wives hired me to chain you
          guys up.

Dick grabs his coat collar, twists it tightly.

                    DICK
          So, you're the one that tipped off
          the wives. Traitor!

                    MC'CORKLE
          I broke my vow. I deserve to die,
          but let me make things right. I
          must be a bum. I got the right
          stuff. Let me help you rescue
          Donny.

A few snowflakes fall.

                    CLIFF
          We got nothin' to lose, Dick. Let
          him go. If he wasn't a true bum
          he wouldn't have told you.

                    MC'CORKLE
          Forgive me. I have sinned against
          my brother bums. I repent and I
          shall save Donny from the fires of
          matrimony.

                    DICK
          We ought to abandon you. You
          defiled the vows. You took an
          oath. How dare you wear the
          medallion? Take it off.

Cliff grabs Dick's wrist. Dick releases his grip, tears off
Mc'Corkle's medallion. Snow falls heavier.

                    DICK
                    (continuing)
          When Donny is saved, you get it
          back.

Mc'Corkle walks down the lonely track alone. Dick stares.
Mc'Corkle fades in the snowstorm.

                    DICK
                 (continuing)
          A good bum wouln't have done what
          he done.

EXT. R.R. TRACKS / BLUE CANYON - DAY

FRANK and HARRY hitchhike in snowdrifts. Spreader and engine
rounds corner driving snow off tracks. Snow sprays and
encapsulates Frank and Harry.

Their heads poke from snow drift. Rotary plow, belches snow,
rounds corner. They hop on. Warm hands by boiler. IRON FACE
tosses Frank and Harry into a snow drift head-first by the,
"Naked Man Saloon." Feet flailing.

                    IRON FACE
          New policy. No bums allowed.

Frank and Harry stand, brush snow from clothes.

                    HARRY
          Ol' Iron Face! Goin' too far,
          Frank. He's takin' on the bums.
          If this keeps up bums be banned
          from the rails forever. We can't
          let it happen, Frank. He's
          breaking the regulations. We got
          rights!

INT. NAKED MAN SALOON - DAY

FRANK and HARRY enter swinging doors. Naked men sit at bar
and tables, some stand by fireplace.

                    NAKED BOUNCER
                 (to Frank, and Harry)
          Off with the clothing or get out.

Grudgingly, they strip. Frank steps to bar phone.

                    VOICE ON PHONE (V.O.)
          Traffic control.

                    FRANK
          Connect me to, Sam Simmons.

                    VOICE ON PHONE (V.O.)
          I can't do that. Get off the
          emergency line.

                        FRANK
            This is Judge Frank Wiener,
            Supreme court. Put Sam on the
            line.

                        VOICE ON PHONE (V.O.)
            Judge Wiener? Oh. Please hold.
                    (beat)
            He's at camp. May I leave a
            message?

                        FRANK
            I know where it is.

                        BUM AT CARD TABLE
                    (to Bartender)
            Hey, throw more wood in the fire.
            It's chilly in here!

Harry's in gift shop b.g. tries out new hobo sticks and
burlap bags, looks in mirror. They leave.

EXT. NAKED MAN SALOON - DAY

FRANK and HARRY trudge through snow drifts, look down at a
colossal geodesic dome in a Ponderosa valley. They carry
their hobo sticks over shoulder.

INT. CAMP FANTASY / GEODESIC DOME - DAY

Casino with hot tubs, video games, bowling alley, roller
coaster, FEMALE ROBOTS massage bums. Drunken BUMS stagger
everywhere.

FRANK and HARRY slip hobo sticks and coats to cloakroom
attendant, approach SAM SIMMONS in hot tub. Robots dangle
grapes over Simmons.

                        FRANK
            Sam Simmons, you ol'tycoon.

                        SIMMONS
            Frank, Harry. Hop in. The
            water's fine.

                        HARRY
            We got problems on the road.

                        SIMMONS
            On my road?

                    FRANK
          Our world is at risk of discovery.
          Iron Face, violating contract of
          1862. "Avowed registered bums
          shall be unmolested to ride
          without fee. No railroad employee
          shall deny a bum's pursuit of
          happiness to live on railroad
          domain."

                    HARRY
          It's the Constitution at stake
          here, Sam. If we take it to court
          to enforce it the publicity will --

Female robot with drinks, smiles at Harry.

                    SIMMONS
          Publicity? No way! My wife
          thinks I'm on a business
          convention. If she finds out it
          will -

                    FRANK
          Be the end of our world. Everyone
          will quit their jobs. Thousands
          will swarm the rails. The economy
          will collapse. No freight to
          ship, trains don't run. With no
          railroad earnings stockholders
          will demand extraordinary expenses
          be paid in dividends. No more
          Camp Fantasy, Sam.

Robot returns, pinches Harry's butt.

                    HARRY
          All of our resorts will be shut
          down. True bums need you, Sam.
          The attitude is spreadin' like
          wildfire. Iron Face threw us off
          the rotary plow. Bums can't use
          switch heaters. Soon he'll be
          tossing our luxury cars off the
          tracks.

Simmons rubs forehead. Harry walks off with robot.

EXT. SIDE OF CLIFF / DONNER PASS - DAY

IRON FACE pushes flaming "Kumquat Juice" boxcar over
embankment. Crumples below into ravine.

BACK TO SCENE

SIMMONS stands, dripping wet, wears G-string. Places arm
around FRANK. Robot in b.g. slaps HARRY. He returns to
Frank. Simmons races to phone at bar. Slams phone.

                         SIMMONS
                    (to Frank and Harry)
               It's not, Iron Face. It's a bum
               gone bad, in Washington.

                         HARRY
               Washington? No! No!

                         SIMMONS
               Congress declined to give him his
               medallion. Refused to let him
               take his vows.

                         FRANK
               Oh, gosh. Political bums.
               They'll screw-up everything. We
               can't let them in.

                         SIMMONS
               Times are changing. Ain't like
               the good ol' days. He's got us by
               the spike. I'm afraid we'll have
               to make concessions. It's the only
               thing we can do to save ourselves.

Robot returns, smiles. Harry steps behind Frank.

                         FRANK
               I can call Chief Justice Byron.
               He's my --

                         SIMMONS
               Government has the right to option
               imminent domain to take over the
               railroad. We could end up being --

                         HARRY
               Amtak? We'd all have to pay!
               Nobody can ride free. It'll ruin
               us!

Robot picks up Harry by crotch, carries him upstairs.

                         HARRY
                    (continuing)
               Frank, help! Help!

Frank turns to assist. Simmons grabs his arm.

                          SIMMONS
                       (to Frank)
                 She's a little frisky, but he'll
                 be okay. Harry needs this.

EXT. WHITE HOUSE / WASHINGTON DC - DAY

Swearing in PRESIDENT. Congressional assembly agitated.

                          PRESIDENT
                 I solemnly swear to be a good bum.
                 To execute my duties for the
                 betterment of all mankind. I will
                 uphold the Constitution of
                 eighteen-sixty-two.

EXT. SANTA'S VILLAGE / CISCO - NIGHT

Sugarcoated gingerbread houses, snowmen, eight reindeers pull
sleds, one with red nose. ELVES roam the streets. Christmas
lights strung everywhere. GP-60M's arrive. Elves SING
Christmas carols by tracks.

INT. GP-60M ENGINE CAB - NIGHT

WIVES amazed, see Christmas village. DONNY tied up on floor
of engine cab. ELVES see wives, SCREAM, run away.

                          YVONNE
                 Those little bums.

                          CHRISTINE
                 And to think we created them for
                 the children.

                          DEBBIE
                 The bums stole Christmas. They
                 want it all for themselves.

SANTA CLAUSE exits home with shotgun. Fires at the engines.
Pellets crack windows, wives duck to floor.

EXT. SANTA'S VILLAGE / FRONT STEPS - NIGHT

                          SANTA
                 Scram, get out of here. I know
                 when you've been bad. No women
                 allowed in my village. Sic'em
                 Rudolf.

ELVES toss candy cane flash grenades BOOM! BOOM! RUDOLF's
nose glows as he dashes up steps, enters cab.

BACK TO SCENE

RUDOLF flashes razor sharp canine teeth GROWLS, tears WIVES
clothes. Hooves stomp on DONNY.

One lands on chin, then groin. Rudolf GROWLS. Wives against
wall. Rudolf pulls Donny's pant leg, drags him out of cab
into the snow.

>   DONNY
>   Help me, Christine. He's going to
>   eat me. Help!

>   CHRISTINE
>   Drag him into the woods, Rudolf.
>   Do what comes natural.

>   DONNY
>   I love you, Christine. Help me.
>   I'll renew our marriage vows.

>   CHRISTINE
>   You promise? Will you renounce
>   your vows to these bums?

>   DONNY
>   I can't.

SANTA fires shotgun again. Herd of reindeers stampede to
train. Wives notch throttle, take off. Reindeers SNARLING
behind train.

INT. GP-60M CAB - NIGHT

ELF leaps on CHRISTINE's back. She flings him out the door
head- first into a snowman. SNOWMEN are BUMS in disguise and
run away.

EXT. WALKWAY TO SANTA'S HOME - NIGHT

>   SANTA
>   Dasher, Dancer, Prancer, Vixen,
>   Comet, Cupid, Donner, Blitzen,
>   cease. C'mere boys!

Deers return. ELVES help DONNY into,

INT. SANTA'S WORKSHOP - NIGHT

Expensive toys on assembly lines, Ferrari, yacht, Rolex
watches, home theater systems, etc.

>   SANTA
>   Gifts for good bums. We're behind
>   schedule. I'm afraid we'll have
>   to put you to work.

>   DONNY
>   Work? I'm on vacation. I don't
>   want to work.

                        SANTA
          A good bum would have volunteered.
                    (to Elves)
          Away with him. Put him in the
          stables with, you know who!

                        ELF
          Snowman's abominable when he's in
          the mood. He trashed the stables
          again, ripped Dancer's antler off.
          I can't get near him to inoculate
          sedatives.

Donny's eyes wide. Sees DANCER with broken horn.

                        SANTA
          One night will kill'm.

                        DONNY
          Okay, okay. I'll work!

                        SANTA
          You better be good and you better
          not pout. Now get to work. We're
          behind schedule.

EXT. R.R. TRACK BY SANTA'S VILLAGE - NIGHT

GP-60M's stopped. DEBBIE pulls switch lever. Track switched.
Engines power up, head for Santa's village. CRASH!

BACK TO SCENE

GP-60's smash through wall crushing expensive gifts.
CHRISTINE tackles DONNY. YVONNE kicks shotgun out of SANTA'S
reach. Reindeers run. Yvonne pulls Santa's beard, drags him
on floor.

                        YVONNE
          There ain't gonna be no Christmas
          unless you tell me where my
          husband is!

ELF on portable Cinderella toy phone.

                        ELF
          Help! Wives in the North Pole.

DEBBIE chases Elf among the wreckage. Finally, lassoes him
with Christmas light cord. Wraps him up tight. Plugs cord
in, elf lights up. ELF in b.g. hides under a gift, speaks on
toy phone.

INT. SD-40 ENGINE CAB / COLD STREAM CANYON - NIGHT

BUM ENGINEER slams phone, notches throttle to full bore #8
slot. Engines step up.

Approaching train on adjacent track descends "S" curves.

                    ENGINEER
          Trouble in paradise.

                    FIREMAN
          Women. They think Christmas was
          made just for them and for kids.
          What about us?

                    ENGINEER
          I don't understand women. Seems
          if a man is happy, must be
          something wrong with the
          relationship, so they pick a fight
          or do something to irritate us.

                    FIREMAN
          Why do they want all the gifts?

                    ENGINEER
          Most jealous creatures in the
          universe.

EXT./ INT. CAMP FANTASY - NIGHT

SD-40's pull in. BUMS exit box cars, enter Camp Fantasy.
ENGINEER and FIREMAN run inside to SIMMONS. FRANK and HARRY
play poker. Engineer and fireman race to Simmons.

                    ENGINEER
          Wives! They raided Santa's
          village. Santa's captured! They
          won't give him up 'less they get
          their husbands back. Say they
          captured a bum named, Donny. They
          stole our Christmas, Sam!

                    SIMMONS
          I'll see we get our Christmas. Did
          the bum take his vow?

                    FRANK
          Yeah.

                    SIMMONS
          Okay, go to red alert.

                    HARRY
          Are you sure?

Crowd of BUMS assemble around them.

                    SIMMONS
          The wives have gone too far. I
          can't run a blasted railroad with
          women disrupting my road. I'll
          lose my status if I don't deliver
          Christmas.

Bums appear sad, then angry.

                    FRANK
          If we don't get those wives off
          the rails we'll lose everything.

                    HARRY
               (to Frank, scolding)
          I thought Dick was gonna do the
          right thing? Ya gotta stop
          invitin' these city bums. They
          ain't cut to be a hobo, never mind
          a bum! Now look what ya'done.

EXT. ROSEVILLE / DEPOT YARD - NIGHT

POOKIE and FRED snap seals off boxcars.

                    FRED
          Simmons wants them. Hurry up.

                    POOKIE
          Man, I don't want to go to jail.

                    FRED
          Don't worry. Simmons knows what
          he's doing.
               (to workmen)
          Hurry up and unload those cars.
          Get me some power.

                    THIRD WORKER
          Prime movers arriving.

Ten SD-40 engines arrive. Couple to boxcars KA-BOOM!

EXT. SANTA'S VILLAGE / CISCO - NIGHT

Engines surround the village. Boxcar doors open, BUMS sneak
to Santa's home, peek in windows. MC'CORKLE jumps, feet-
first down chimney, fire extinguisher in both hands.

INT. SANTA'S VILLAGE - NIGHT

DONNY hangs by ropes from ceiling. CHRISTINE holds a burning
marshmallow by his lips. PLOOF! Mc'Corkle lands in
fireplace, sprays CO_2 gas at fire and wives PSSSSSHH!

BUMS charge through the door CRASH-BOOM!

WIVES scramble to Santa's sleigh, whip reindeers, break
through a wall, escape into the night. Mc'Corkle cuts ropes,
lowers Donny. Rope looped around Donny's neck. He can't
breath.

                    DONNY
                 (gasping)
            Mc'Corkle, it was horrible. I
            don't ever want to go back to
            civilization again. I'm a bum and
            I'll always be a bum.

                    MC'CORKLE
            We were born to be bums.

They hug. Angry bums inspect smashed gifts. SANTA comes out
of hiding under yacht with his elves.

                    SANTA
            My sleigh. I can't deliver
            presents without it.

                    BUM
            Merry Christmas, Santa.

They look outside. DICK and CLIFF stand on decorated engine,
tows a sleigh and a string of flatcars loaded with new cars,
jet ski's, snowmobiles, yacht, motorcycles, etc.

                    SANTA
            Ho-ho-ho! Merry Christmas!

Dick gives Mc'Corkle his medallion. They hug. Elves SING.

EXT. DONNER LAKE OVERLOOK - DAY

A huge new red and silver SD-80 engine idles. Long
procession of remorseful BUMS, each holds a dandelion, slowly
step along platform into cab, exit other side without flower.

                    FRANK
            Poor, Casey.

                    HARRY
            He lived a good life, Frank. His
            wife never caught him. A true bum
            he was.

                    DONNY
                 (to Dick)
            What did they do? Make Casey sit
            in the chair?

                    DICK
            Shhh! Just get in line.

They pluck a dandelion, enter cab.

INT. SD-80 ENGINE CAB - DAY

BUMS lay flowers in the nose compartment. A large concrete
block inside, engraved with, "Casey R.I.P. Ride Forever The
Iron Road." They toss flowers on crypt.

                    DICK
               (whispers to Harry)
          What the hell is this? You buried
          him in the engine?

                    HARRY
          All engines require ballast
          counterweight. We entomb our
          fallen ones here in concrete. It
          is the highest honor a true bum
          can hope for.

Dick's brows sink, rubs chin.

                    CLIFF
          I always wondered what was inside
          the pug-nose end of those engines.

                    FRANK
          You are blessed to know these
          secrets. Any engineer will show
          you the crypt. It brings them
          good luck. Many engineers are
          buried inside their locomotives.
          Even celebrities. Their wives may
          think they are in a cemetery, but
          this is a railman's secret. You
          must never tell anyone what you
          have seen today.

Donny's amazed. Touches the crypt. Dick touches Donny's
shoulder, he SCREAMS. BUMS give his scolding looks.

                    DICK
          The thought of Forest Acres gives
          me the chills. Imagine the
          boredom of counting bird droppings
          all day. I want to be free as the
          wind, go places, see the country.
          This is a fantastic way to go.
          How much does it cost?

Dick pulls out his credit card.

                    FRANK
          Money can't buy these plots. Only
          the Federation of Bums in
          Washington determine who will be
          interned. We have a shortage of
          locomotives and a waiting list.

Dick frowns. Folds and tears credit card in half.

                    HARRY
          Honor must be earned. Casey paid
          his dues for over thirty-years.
          You willing to give your youth to
          the rails?

A moment of silence. They all exit cab to,

EXT. BY SD-80 ENGINES - DAY

Engines RUMBLE. Compressed air bursts PSST! Sprays yellow
water on CLIFF's pants. Cliff leaps out of the way. A BUM in
cab grins. Near air pipe, a sign, "Toilet Vent."

DICK in deep thought, shuffles to a small babbling brook.
Cliff dives in, splashes Dick.

                    DICK
               (to himself)
          Why must life be so hard?

HARRY approaches. Places hand on Dick's shoulder. Cliff in
b.g. splashes, cusses. DONNY sees a CROW in tree. He stares,
concerned with its every move.

                    HARRY
          Every action of our lives touches
          a chord that will vibrate in
          eternity. You're not ready to
          live until you are ready to die.
          Casey lived. Come, let us do the
          same.

EXT. CABOOSE / FOREST - DAY

Two story CABOOSE sits on siding. Swirling smoke from
smokestack drifts into forest. It's snowing.

INT. CABOOSE - DAY

WIVES cooking inside. Snow floats by windows.

                    YVONNE
          Believe me. This will work.

                    CHRISTINE
          More onions. They love onions.

                    DEBBIE
          Here's some garlic.

INT. IGLOO BUM ENCAMPMENT / FOREST - DAY

Card room with chandeliers, red carpets, huge roaring
fireplace. BUMS dressed as mountain men play cards.

Two BUMS rub axle grease on boots, smell food.

                        FIRST BUM
             It's only your imagination.

                        SECOND BUM
             But it smells so real. I smell
             onions and garlic, Tramp.

                        TRAMP
             Hoby, the mind plays tricks on you
             when you think of the past.

                        HOBY
             I gotta check it out.

                        TRAMP
             Oh, all right. I'll go with you,
             but I'm telling you it's not real.

EXT. FOREST - DAY

TRAMP and HOBY tread through snowy forest, see caboose.\

                        TRAMP
             It's a mirage. It really doesn't
             exist.

INT. CABOOSE - DAY

HOBEY and TRAMP step inside, see simmering food and eat.
DEBBIE steps from closet, wears neglige, twitches finger to
attract Hoby into a small room. Door closes. YVONNE and
CHRISTINE charge downstairs, capture Tramp.

                        HOBY (V.O.)
                      (soothing)
             Oooh, ahh! Please stop.
                      (pain)
             Yeowch! Help me, Tramp. It's a
             trap!

Tramp opens door, sees Debbie on Hoby's back forcing an
enormous hypodermic needle into his butt. Hoby's arms tied
to bed. Tramp runs, Christine blocks the door.

                        CHRISTINE
             Now my little bum. How would you
             like to show bums? With me!

She's smacks a rolling pin in her palm.

                         YVONNE
              Why suffer? Tell us where our
              husbands are and we'll let you go
              with a picnic basket of goodies.

              Be reasonable. It's the only way
              to save your buddy.

Tramp licks his chops, sees the food. Hoby screams o.s.
Tramp nods, reaches for food. Yvonne grabs wrist.

                         YVONNE
                      (continuing)
              Not one bite 'til you talk.

INT. C44-9W ENGINE CAB - DAY

CHRISTINE drives a stack of ten new orange/black C44-9W
engines. Freight train with four SD-9 engine pushers. WIVES
chase HUSBANDS in Baldwin through mountainous winding
switchbacks.

                         DEBBIE
              They lied to us. Took our food
              too. Be careful, Christine. A
              curve is coming up.

Christine notches throttle back. Wheels SCREECH.

                         YVONNE
              It's no use. These bums have
              taken vows to never betray their
              trust. It's just not worth chasing
              a man who doesn't love you anymore.

INT. BALDWIN ENGINE - TRESTLE BRIDGE - DAY

Baldwin passes over bridge as WIVE's train goes under. TRIO
see their wives. DICK in engineer seat.

                         DICK
                      (to Donny, Cliff,
                       Mc'Corkle)
              Both of you! Shovel coal. I need
              a full head of steam. Move it!

CLIFF and DONNY grudgingly shovel coal into firebox.

BACK TO SCENE

                    CHRISTINE
          But what about revenge? We need
          to get even. They just can't walk
          away without punishment. The
          world would be a mess if it were
          not for retribution. Even the
          scales of justice will be held by
          a man if we don't do something.

They see the THREE MEN in suits hitchhiking. One is black.
They stop the train. Men climb aboard.

                    FIRST MAN
          Good afternoon, ladies.

                    SECOND MAN
          You gals sure are a sight for sore
          eyes. We met in Sacramento
          haven't we?

                    YVONNE
          I believe so.

                    BLACK MAN
          Did you ever find your husbands?

                    YVONNE
          They're here, but we can't catch
          them.

                    FIRST MAN
          Darn fools run away from such
          beautiful women. Why if it were
          me, I'd never leave you, ever.

Wives like what they hear. They smile sheepishly.

INT. BALDWIN ENGINE / NORDEN - DAY

CLIFF at throttle. DICK stands outside on platform by window.

                    DICK
               (to Cliff)
          Cliff, if Casey could only see you
          now he'd be so proud. Give it
          more steam. Listen to her voice,
          kid. We got three minutes to make
          it through the Big Hole before the
          consist arrives. If we miss, it's
          head-on.

                    CLIFF
          I see it. The Big Hole! Give me
          more steam! Donny, get your butt
          to work!

DONNY shovels coal feverishly, GRUMBLES under his breath,

              DONNY
      Slavedriver.

Darkness as they enter the Big Hole tunnel. Exit other side
seeing freight consist approaching.

              DICK
      Yeeoow! It's ahead of schedule.
      One-hundred-percent throttle!

Cliff shoves throttle. Steam gage rises into red zone, 450
p.s.i. Safety valves HISS. Consist triple HORNS blaring.
Dick leaps inside Baldwin cab as consist gets too close.

Baldwin slams into switch, veers left, just in time, but
consist engines smash into watercar, knocks it off track,
tumbles down gorge. Baldwin cylinder head POPS like a
bullet, flips on ground.

              DICK
        (continuing)
      Zero throttle. Full brakes!

Cliff pulls brake lever.

              CLIFF
      It won't budge. We're downhill
      too fast. We got to bail out.

              DICK
      Shut that firedoor. Pressure too
      high. Noooo!

Staybolts SNAP on firesheet, HISSING steam BOOM! Boiler
explodes, jettisons like a rocket, leaves only the truck and
shattered cab racing down hill. Head straight for the
roundhouse. Full panic.

              DICK
        (continuing)
      Hold on! Oh my sweet --

CRASH! Truck slams through roundhouse door,

INT. ROUNDHOUSE - DAY

TRUCK whacks turnstile hard, throws TRIO out of cab. DICK
and CLIFF land by parked engines into bails of hay. A cow
inside MOOS. Chickens and geese SQUAWK and fly.

              DICK
      Everyone okay? Where's Donny?

                              DONNY
                    Ouch! Ouch! I'm up here. Get me
                    off this hot seat.

DONNY sits on smokestack of a HISSING steam locomotive. Hot
black smoke pours around his butt. A flying goose bites
Donny's ear OUCH! Dick helps Donny down. Cliff chases goose
and chickens.

                              DICK
                    We did it! The first bums to ever
                    ride Baldwin's engine against the
                    grain.

                    Why, every bum in the world will
                    respect us now. We earned the
                    right to be epitomed on a ballast
                    to ride the rails forever. Just
                    like, Casey.

Dick smiles. Peeks out doorway, smile dissolves.

                              DICK
                         (continuing)
                    They stopped chasing us.

                              DONNY
                    Thank heavens. We're free at last!

                              CLIFF
                    The consist? What if they hit
                    head-on?

                              DICK
                    We have to go back.

They fire up the steam locomotive, leave roundhouse.

EXT. MOUNTAINS / VERDI / DONNER PASS - DAY

Steam locomotive arcs over a rise. TRIO sees the C44-9W's
idling on siding THUMP! THUMP! THUMP! THUMP!

WIVES sit at picnic bench with the THREE MEN IN SUITS.
Candlelight diner. Freight and Amtak trains pass by.

                              DONNY
                    No wonder. Cheatin' on us! I
                    swear, you must keep them barefoot
                    and chained indoors. They can't
                    be trusted in a man's world.

                              DICK
                    That does it. Women don't have
                    the right to treat us like this.
                    Imagine them wanting freedom. I'll
                    never understand them.

>   CLIFF
>   Let 'em be. It's not worth
>   chasing a woman who doesn't love
>   you. Women turn men into bums.
>   You know it's true.

>   DICK
>   Truth? I'm not letting Yvonne off
>   the hook so easy. I'll make her
>   suffer.

Dick yanks the brakes PSHHHH! Engine chugs to a stop.

EXT. PICNIC TABLE - DAY

The THREE MEN hold WIVES hands. TRIO approaches, steaming
mad. Dick blows out candles.

>   DICK
>   Party's over.

Trio grab wives, toss over shoulder as they kick and scream.

>   WIVES
>   (randomly)
>   "Let me go." "I want to stay here
>   where I'm appreciated and loved."
>   "I refuse to go home." "Get your
>   hands off my tush."

Wives wink to us, smile. Trio haul them onto engine and
steam off under a waterfall into a golden sunset.

The three men by picnic table rip off clothing. They are
WOMEN!

SERIES OF SHOTS

EXT. - DONNER PASS / TRUCKEE - SUNSET

- - Snow falls in a mountain meadow pass. SD-40'S pass by.
MC'CORKLE in cab, waves. Entire train strung with Christmas
lights, candy canes, etc.

- - Flatcar squeaks by. SANTA and ELVES in the sleigh wave.
FRANK and HARRY open gifts. Santa and Elves toss gifts into
the snow, "Ho-ho-ho! Merry Christmas!"

- - BUMS with their WIVES on passing flatcar stand by a
campfire, SING Christmas carols. IRON FACE pouts.

- - Private car glides by. Three EXECUTIVES and WIVES wave.
Including SIMMONS and the United States PRESIDENT. They tear
open gifts on rear platform, expensive clothes, jewelry.

- - Flatcar nativity scene passes us by. SKINNER and JASPER dressed as wise men sit on camels, wave.

- - TOM and DARLENE, ROGER and KAREN sit by boxcar doorway,
linking together gold waist chains, kissing. Banner above,
"Just Married."

- - Caboose trails smoke from chimney. CHARLOTTE and ELISE
hold hands with FRED and POOKIE, wave and yell, "Merry
Christmas." Toss gifts into snow banks.

- - A NURSE leaps off train as it rumbles downhill. Lonely
BUMS stroll out of the woods in snowshoes, open gifts in the
snow. CASEY and SPARKY opens gifts, smile, gold "TB"
medallion. Nurse SCREAMS, chases Casey.

-- DICK, DONNY, CLIFF with their WIVES roll by on adjacent
track. Dick tosses a gift. NURSE and ANOTHER WOMAN chase
CASEY and SPARKY onto the coalcar. They SCREAM throw coal at
the men.

                    WOMAN
          Fakin' your dead, huh? Get over
          here, Casey.

-- Camera boom drops into frame, SPELLBOUND behind camera.

                    SPELLBOUND
          That's a wrap.

He steps out of boom, runs to the gift Dick tossed, opens it.
Inside - Oscar with card attached.

ON CARD

                    DICK'S VOICE (V.O.)
          Merry Christmas! I told you so.
          Truly a bum always, Dick.

                              FADE OUT:

          The End.

THE 7 DAY PLAN TO BE A BETTER CHRISTIAN!

SUNDAY -- This is a day of rest (see Saturday) of which no work is to be performed. Take full advantage of it! However, extend extra kindness to others. Read the Word, listen to Christian radio and watch TV for faith comes by "hearing" the Word of God.

MONDAY -- Drive your vehicle with patience towards others. Be changed at work. No more gossip, complaining, bad jokes. Just start being nice -- Biblically correct! Be cooperative. Can you do this for just one day?

TUESDAY -- Forget Me! Do a good thing for another. Open doors, buy someone a meal or gift, feed a stranger's parking meter. Give so you will receive. Give something! The Lord gives, so should you.

WEDNESDAY -- Compliment Day! Say something nice to someone, including one who may not like you. Be sincere about it! If someone needs help, go to their aid. Make someone smile today!

THURSDAY -- Distribute a Bible track. No tracks? Make or buy some! It is time you begin your ministry to the Lord to share the Good News. There are many hurting people who need the Lord and it is your responsibility to introduce them to Him. Using tracks make the job easy!

FRIDAY -- Day of forgiveness! When you forgive others transgressions, you are released from the anguish within yourself. It is easy to do! Start the process today! See Tuesday and Wednesday's instructions. Life is so much easier to live and great mercy and blessing arrive when you forgive!

SATURDAY -- Rest if this is the Sabbath you honor or donate; time, items, food, or money to the homeless shelters. Do not forget the poor! Visit or call a relative or friend. Express your appreciation for what the Lord has given you! Share with others what you have and the Lord will give you even more!

Free Bible Tracks For SASE!   Contact Us For Bible Tracks!

EACH DAY

START the day right by greeting the Lord and giving thanks for all He has done and what He will do for you in the future. **END** the day right by expressing your gratitude to the Lord.

SPEAK often to the Lord, as he is your best friend. Remember, he wants to handle every detail in your life, even the small stuff. Do not become so busy in your day you leave Him out of your life.

WHEN you pray just speak as you would to a friend. There is no need for theatrical displays of emotions or insincerity. If you fall short, do not turn your face away from the Lord and hide. Take the issue to Him.

WHAT will you give to the Lord if He grants your request? Will you simply say thank you and forget Him until you need something else later? The Lord sees the suffering of the sick and poor. Why not pledge to help them? Make your promise and keep it! Do it now before you recieve. This is faith in action.

SPREAD the Word of God. You may not be a minister, but you can distribute tracks. Leave them everywhereyou go. Keep some on your person each day. Your reward shall be great! Write us for tracts!

TITHE to the Lord. Give and you shall recieve more! Give to churches, ministries, homeless shelters, or where there is dire need. A perfect expression of love for others! God's System Never Fails!

PRINT AND DISTRIBUTE TO OTHERS!

JAMES RUSSELL PUBLISHING

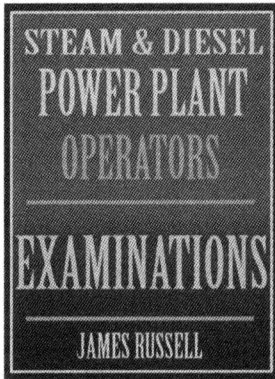

www.ingramcontent.com/pod-product-compliance
Lightning Source LLC
Chambersburg PA
CBHW081153090426
42736CB00017B/3303